"We are all made better when we face the truth. John Dickerson delivers a clear, compelling case for why the church must reform or face the natural consequence of fading influence. He doesn't just urge us to wake up, he gives the church clear direction for the days ahead. A brilliant book. A must read for any Christian hoping to see their faith regain traction in a changing world."

—Gabe Lyons, author of *The Next Christians*
and Founder of Q Ideas

"John Dickerson is that rarity among evangelicals—a journalist of the highest capacity, but more than that, an analyst of breadth, insight, and laser-sharp foresight. With persuasive force, his book portrays the future status and functioning of the church in a national culture that is alienated from Christianity. Few writers can gather, process, distill, and apply a host of facts with the precision of John Dickerson."

—John McCandlish Phillips, veteran *New York Times*
journalist and author

"An important book that every believer should not only read but heed."

—Cal Thomas, *USA Today* columnist
and Fox News personality

"John Dickerson has pulled together some sobering statistics and laid out a biblical game plan for dealing with the inevitable cultural changes that lie ahead. These aren't changes that might occur. They are changes that have occurred (the horse-is-already-out-of-the-barn-type changes). I would encourage every Christian leader to read, ponder, and consider the facts and the strategies John presents in *The Great Evangelical Recession*. It will help prepare you for the future."

—Larry Osborne, pastor and author,
North Coast Church, Vista, CA

"Nobody likes getting a bad diagnosis—whether it's medical, financial, or spiritual. But once we get past the reality that things aren't the way we thought they were, we're actually in the best position to turn our circumstances around for the good. John Dickerson's workup on the health and welfare of the evangelical cause may jolt your spiritual senses, but he's followed it up with a prescription that will work. There's no gloom or doom in *The Great Evangelical Recession*—just an honest assessment of where we are and solid hope for what we need to do to get to where we need to be."

—Dr. Tim Kimmel, author of *Grace-Based Parenting* and *In Praise of Plan B*

"*The Great Evangelical Recession* has gone a long way in contextualizing the plight of the church in today's culture. There is no question that the church has weakened over these last few decades, and before we can expect our Lord to bring healing and revitalization to its health, there must be a humble truthfulness to our condition. John Dickerson's work has served us well in bringing sense to what brought us to this point and providing honest reflection upon it. I believe we could once again see a dynamic and powerful witness to our world from believers honoring their Lord and bringing glory to their heavenly Father."

—Dr. Darryl DelHousaye, president of Phoenix Seminary

THE GREAT
EVANGELICAL
RECESSION

THE GREAT
EVANGELICAL
RECESSION

6 Factors That Will
Crash the American Church
. . . and How to Prepare

JOHN S. DICKERSON

BakerBooks
a division of Baker Publishing Group
Grand Rapids, Michigan

Published by Baker Books
a division of Baker Publishing Group
P.O. Box 6287, Grand Rapids, MI 49516-6287
www.bakerbooks.com

Printed in the United States of America

Library of Congress Cataloging-in-Publication Data
Dickerson, John S.
    The great evangelical recession : 6 factors that will crash the American church—and how to prepare / John S. Dickerson.
        p.   cm.
    Includes bibliographical references.
    ISBN 978-0-8010-1483-3 (pbk. : alk. paper)
    1. United States—Church history—21st century. 2. Evangelicalism—United States. 3. United States—Social conditions—21st century. 4. United States—Civilization—21st century. I. Title.
BR526.D48 2013
277.3'083—dc23   2012034291

All emphasis, shown by italics, in Scripture is the author's.

Unless otherwise indicated, Scripture quotations are from the HOLY BIBLE, NEW INTERNATIONAL VERSION®. Copyright © 1973, 1978, 1984 Biblica. Used by permission of Zondervan. All rights reserved.

Scripture quotations identified GW are from GOD'S WORD®. © 1995 God's Word to the Nations. Used by permission of Baker Publishing Group.

Cover design by Kathleen Lynch of Black Kat Design

Author is represented by Ambassador Literary Agency

13   14   15   16   17   18   19   7   6   5   4   3   2   1

To my bride, who loves me despite my flaws.
And to Christ, who loves His bride despite hers.

Contents

Introduction

The Great Recession

Be sure you know the condition of your flocks,
give careful attention to your herds;
for riches do not endure forever,
and a crown is not secure for all generations.

Proverbs 27:23–24

What if somebody had warned us ten years ago that a "Great Recession" would throw the world's largest banks into bankruptcy? That the U.S. stock market would lose half its value? That one in six Americans would be on food stamps while 100,000 homes foreclose each month? In the glory years of the early 2000s, as homes were gaining tens of thousands in value each year, would anyone have believed such predictions?

What if, in the 1980s, after the launch of the wildly successful *USA Today*, somebody had predicted that leading newspapers and magazines would be insolvent within three presidencies? That the *Chicago Tribune* would file Chapter 11, the *Rocky Mountain News* would close its doors, or that *Newsweek* would sell its operations for $1?

The reality is that in each of these great collapses, there were isolated observers who did see the writing on the wall—and did attempt to warn the key players.

In 2005, when housing prices were climbing with apparent invincibility, I interviewed one such doomsday prophet for *The Scottsdale Times*. Michael Pollack, an Arizona real estate investor worth about $1 billion, told me that within years the real estate industry would flip upside down. Even as home values were increasing monthly, he said to sell soon, before the market turned.

The problem with the Great Recession wasn't that nobody saw it coming. The problem was that the people who needed to listen, to put on the brakes, to adjust course, never got the message. Or else they ignored it.

The American church stands today in a similar position, on the precipice of a great evangelical recession. While we focus on a few large churches and dynamic national leaders, the church's overall numbers are shrinking. Its primary fuel—donations—is drying up and disappearing. And its political fervor is dividing the movement from within. In addition to these internal crises, the outside host culture is quietly but quickly turning antagonistic and hostile toward evangelicals.

The signposts are obvious, but many of the leaders who most need to see and plan for these trends are too busy to notice the broad cultural shifts. Others are too deceived by current success to believe that industries and ministries, like governments, can topple almost overnight in the fast-paced 21st century.

Around the globe, cultures are changing faster and with more complexity than ever before. Just as the printing press accelerated cultural change during the Reformation and Renaissance, personal 24/7 web access is now accelerating cultural change beyond what even the cable television generation expects. Trends that would have taken years to evolve in the 20th century can now affect the culture and its industries in days or hours.

International revolutions during the Arab Spring of 2011 toppled decades-old governments. These revolts of thousands were organized via technologies that did not even exist six years earlier—Twitter and Facebook, among others.

As George Friedman writes in his forecast, *The Next 100 Years*, "It is simply that the things that appear to be so permanent and dominant at any given moment in history can change with stunning rapidity. Eras come and go."[1]

Whether in ministry or in industry, those who observe and embrace this new, rapid speed of change become survivors and innovators. Those who ignore the change—and the speed of it—become its victims.

Strategic Thinkers Needed

A prudent man sees danger and takes refuge, but the simple keep going and suffer for it.

Proverbs 22:3

In 2005, New York University economics professor Nouriel Roubini warned that home prices were riding a speculative wave that would soon sink the economy.[2]

One year later, while home prices were still skyrocketing, he told world finance leaders at the International Monetary Fund that the "United States was likely to face a once-in-a-lifetime housing bust, an oil shock, sharply declining consumer confidence, and, ultimately, a deep recession. He laid out a bleak sequence of events: homeowners defaulting on mortgages, trillions of dollars of mortgage-backed securities unraveling worldwide and the global financial system shuddering to a halt."[3]

Some laughed at Roubini's warning. Some shrugged. Most ignored him altogether. His dire forecasts earned him the nickname Dr. Doom, a slight that nearly sank his career until his predictions started manifesting live on CNN, Fox News, and, before long, in our own home values, investment portfolios, and businesses.

Had Roubini's warning been taken to heart, thousands of jobs, homes, and companies could have been saved—even though the broader economic recession was unstoppable at that point.

Similarly, the Great Evangelical Recession is, in some ways, unstoppable today. But ministries and leaders who adjust course now can prepare to survive the coming decades—and even thrive in a changing future. Leaders who prepare now can better steward the resources, staff, and souls God has entrusted to them. The church *as we know it* will face great upheaval, but Christ's kingdom will continue advancing. Leaders who do not position themselves as part of the advance will be victims of the evangelical recession.

The findings in this book are based on fact, not hunch. Still, I write them knowing that some will laugh. Some will shrug, and others will ignore them. It won't be the first time that bad news gets ignored in the church. In his article "A Wakeup Call for Evangelicals," Tom Sine writes that thirty years ago he warned mainline denominational leaders about frightening statistics in their movement, to no avail. He now sees the same trends hitting evangelicalism.

> When I attempted to make leaders in mainline denominations aware of emerging patterns of decline in attendance in the 1980s, they were largely in denial. Denominational leaders today are faced with the continuing crisis of numbers of attendance and giving that are declining every year. Now evangelical denominations are also beginning to experience decline. Twenty-three of twenty-five major evangelical denominations, including the Southern Baptist Convention, are experiencing declining attendance patterns.[4]

Tom Sine's warnings, like Roubini's, were not ignored because his facts were incomplete. Nor were they brushed aside for lack of credentials. Roubini and Sine were ignored because we do not like to hear bad news, especially when it affects us personally. That same fear will blind some to the findings in this book. Fear will cause them to ignore or discount the facts.

On one hand, present success clouds our judgment about what could be happening beyond our line of sight. On the other hand, even in times of success, most of us are overwhelmed. We struggle daily with our own finances, calendars, families, and in-boxes. Who wants to hear about *more* problems? Who wants to hear that things may get worse? I once pitched the content in one of these chapters to a national evangelical magazine. A senior editor replied that the findings, while serious and true, are not the kind of bad news his customers want to read.

Roubini was also overlooked because his conclusion contradicted dozens, no, hundreds of other economists and "experts." How could all those experts have missed what Roubini saw so clearly? Answer: They were too close to the data, too much in the action, and too vested in the conclusions.

Distance often brings perspective. When I worked full-time as a secular journalist—active in the evangelical church but not em-ployed by it—these observations came with ease and clarity. The deeper I move into the movement, now serving as a senior pastor and working from the inside, the less I want to believe that these trends are in play. Unfortunately, while my emotions have changed, the facts have not. If anything, being embedded in the movement has only confirmed the urgency for making these findings known.

In a day of specialists and complexity, very few observers have the ability—like Roubini—to see the big picture in any industry. The same is true in ministry. One specialist can speak on this dy-namic or that factor, this report or that statistic. But very few are trained or gifted or bold enough to look and see the whole monster.

Marcus Buckingham and Donald Clifton of the Gallup orga-nization call thinkers like Roubini "strategic." They identify this inherent ability in their research-based book *Now, Discover Your Strengths*.

> The Strategic theme enables you to sort through the clutter and find the best route. It is not a skill that can be taught. It is a dis-tinct way of thinking, a special perspective on the world at large. This perspective allows you to see patterns where others simply see complexity.[5]

People are either strategic thinkers or they are not. It can't be trained. Roubini was and is a strategic thinker. Where other

economists saw complexity, he saw patterns. From those patterns
he reached conclusions. Disturbing conclusions that seemed im-
plausible at the time.

The authors add, "Mindful of these patterns, [the Strategic
Thinker will] play out alternative scenarios, always asking, 'What
if this happened?'"[6]

This book is essentially the playing out of one such scenario:
"What if the course of the evangelical mainstream does *not* make
a radical change in the next fifteen years? What if the patterns of
fewer new believers, more quitters, decreasing giving, political
infighting, and a growing hostility from the host culture all continue?" And secondly, "If those factors do continue, how does a
successful leader position her or his ministry to survive and thrive?"

Together we will examine these trends through studies and reports from dozens of researchers and specialists—some within the
church and some without. We will investigate the factors that are
challenging the church *as we know it*, and then we will attempt to
foresee where an unchanged evangelical church might be in fifteen
or twenty-five years. As George Barna predicts,

> The church landscape will continue to evolve into something that
> would have been unrecognizable a quarter century ago. . . . The
> mainline churches and even some of the evangelical and fundamen-
> talist groups that were solid at the end of the last millennium and
> the beginning of this one will lose altitude unless they substantially
> reinvent themselves.[7]

We can reinvent ourselves ten years from now, in desperate reaction. Or we can reinvent ourselves now, in thoughtful proactive
planning. Prepared ministry leaders *can* thrive in the 21st century
by adjusting course and applying God's truth to these trends.

Incidentally, drawing simple factual conclusions from boxes
of data was my specialty as a journalist. In 2008 I summarized
the state of Arizona's oversight of twenty thousand physicians
in three investigative stories. Those stories caught the attention
of Tom Brokaw, Charles Gibson, and other news industry leaders from *Newsweek*, the *Chicago Tribune,* and the *New Yorker*.

They named the series winner of the national Livingston Award for Young Journalists, a prize that pits the best journalists from the *New York Times*, the *Wall Street Journal*, CNN, Fox News, NPR, and every other news outlet all against each other.

This project is a much taller effort. It aims to summarize and make sense of the evangelical mainstream—again, not from hunch or opinion, but from the research of dozens of experts. It then aims to cradle the findings in prayer and Scripture and present them with the heart of a pastor—all in hopes that evangelical leaders will work together to become more forward thinking and forward praying, for God's glory and kingdom.

What follows is not depressing. It simply tests our loyalty. While confronting these facts, we will be forced to answer, again and again, "Am I more committed to evangelicalism *as we know it*, or to Jesus Christ, His kingdom, and His message?"

Christ's church has always faced change. Through it all, He has promised, "I will build my church, and the gates of Hades will not overcome it" (Matthew 16:18). Christianity *as we know it* is receding. The evangelical recession offers us a window of opportunity, during which we can re-center Christ's church on *His* mission. Wise leaders must be aware of what is changing, why it's changing, and how to prepare. I take heart in these recent words from a young evangelical leader, Gabe Lyons:

> I believe this moment is unlike any other time in history. Its uniqueness demands an original response. If we fail to offer a different way forward, we risk losing entire generations to apathy and cynicism. Our friends will continue to drift away, meeting their need for spiritual transcendence through other forms of worship and communities of faith that may be less true but more authentic and appealing.[8]

The second part of this book, chapters 7–12, cast the vision for a "different way" forward in the American church. These chapters may be this book's most practical contribution to your ministry. Important as journalistic research about the church is, it does us no good unless it propels us closer to Christ and His Word. And so, for each trend or "problem" identified in the first six chapters, you will find a correlating "solution" given in the final chapters.

Spiritually, these solutions are the meat of this book. They are, I believe, bold, fresh, and firmly biblical. This book does not point to my own church or any other human model as the solution to our decline. It points to the Head of the church as our only "living hope" in a time of great spiritual conflict.

In that sense, the latter chapters are most important. Research can open our eyes to the true state of the church, but God alone through Scripture can inform our hearts as to how we must correct course. My prayer is that God uses this book to draw you closer to His heart, "so that the body of Christ may be built up" (Ephesians 4:12).

A deep love for Christ's bride in the United States drives this project. May these observations prepare you and thousands of others to better lead, better serve, and better be Christ's physical presence in this nation and around the world, as 21st-Century Evangelicals.

Gregory Elder tells a story that illustrates my optimistic hope for the church in the face of real and underestimated adversity.

Growing up on the Atlantic Coast, I spent long hours working on intricate sand castles; whole cities would appear beneath my hands. One year, for several days in a row, I was accosted by bullies who smashed my creations. Finally I tried an experiment: I placed cinder blocks, rocks, and chunks of concrete in the base of my castles. Then I built the sand kingdoms on top of the rocks. When the local toughs appeared (and I disappeared), their bare feet suddenly met their match. Many people see the church in grave peril from a variety of dangers: secularism, politics, heresies, or plain old sin. They forget that the church is built upon a Rock, over which the gates of hell itself shall not prevail.[9]

Part One

Six Trends of Decline

1

Inflated

Think of yourself with sober judgment.

Romans 12:3

Here's the first thing we need to understand about the Great Evangelical Recession: The evangelical church in the United States is not nearly as large as we've been told. This might not seem like a big deal, but it's a huge deal.

The economic recession—with all its foreclosed homes, layoffs, bankruptcies, international unrest, and demolished nest eggs—began with one simple, consistent overestimation. A chorus of forces slowly and steadily inflated the prices of homes in the United States.[1] Prices ballooned far beyond the true values of homes.

We've seen what happened as a result. World economies contracted. The U.S. stock market lost half its value. Millions lost their jobs. Millions more lost their life savings. Many still haven't found new jobs, and many who were retiring are now working into their sixties and seventies.

Overestimating the size and "value" of the evangelical church is—much like housing prices—one of the silent triggers, one of the unexamined fault lines under the Great Evangelical Recession.

In a moment, I'll explain just how much we have overestimated our size. But first, a word on why it matters. In the coming chapters, we're going to see irrefutable data. We'll see that . . .

- the fuel of American evangelicalism—dollars—is disappearing and will dwindle over the next three decades.
- we're losing millions of our own people—about 2.6 million per decade, just from one generation studied.
- the evangelical church is not winning new believers fast enough to keep pace with rapid population growth in the United States.
- while these forces eat at the church internally, the external climate is turning against evangelicals. The fastest growing subcultures in the United States express a militant antagonism against Christians who take the Bible seriously.
- what's left of a smaller, shrinking, strapped church is also splintering and splitting itself over politics and postmodern views of God and the Bible.

We are piecing these massive, moving trends together, into one megatrend. The megatrend reveals a trajectory of massive regression—far larger than the simple sum of the parts. The decline of evangelical Christianity is not *just* that we're failing at evangelism or *just* that we're failing to keep our own kids or *just* that we'll lose 70 percent of our funding in the next thirty years. It's all those factors (and more) combined and gaining speed simultaneously.

Here's why knowing the size of the evangelical church is so important. The question is not, is United States evangelicalism gaining altitude or losing it? The question is, since all these trends are downward, how much altitude can we lose before crashing?

If evangelicals make up half of the United States population—as many of us have been told—these trends might not cost us any sleep. If half the United States is evangelical, the 2.6 million people we lost last decade account for about 2 percent of the church.

On the other hand, if the evangelical church is only about 22 million Americans, as a growing crowd of respected sociologists estimate—well, if that's the case, then we lost more than 10 percent of our people in the last ten years. That's worth losing sleep over. It's worth noticing. If this size and loss are accurate, then we must rethink what we're doing, why we're doing it, and how we're going about it.

So, the crass bumper sticker is right: "Size matters."

Whether it's this book or the next church study to land a *USA Today* headline, we can't make sense of new data if we don't know how big or small the national church actually is. We need a baseline—a rough estimate of where we're starting from, so we can gauge and interpret new trends.

Let me illustrate how a big-picture, foundational understanding helps us make sense of new information. You've probably seen a headline like this one: "America's 100 Largest Churches Doubled in Size During the Decade!"[2]

We might read a headline like that and assume that evangelicalism is doubling, or at least increasing, according to the latest study. But, an understanding of larger trends tells us that at least three in four of those "new" attendees left another church to attend the growing megachurch.[3] In other words, the majority of that "growth" is not growth but transfer of existing evangelicals. More importantly, an understanding of the grand scheme informs us that total attendance at all evangelical churches is declining in almost every state, according to researchers who track combined attendance across all churches in the United States.

So, aware of those foundational facts, we interpret the same exclamatory headline to mean that more people are leaving smaller churches to attend larger ones—even as the total number of folks attending any evangelical church slowly declines.

The great news of the report becomes unremarkable and expected, because we zoomed out to the broader landscape of foundational facts. The opposite is true, too. Armed with an understanding of the grand scheme, some studies will be unexpected and remarkable.

So we begin our exploration by establishing a broad understanding. In this case, we determine the approximate size of the evangelical church in the United States. Chalking this plumb line will help us make sense of dozens of other studies and statistics.

What We're Measuring and Why It Matters

What exactly are we measuring? In this book we are examining "evangelical" Christians and the national evangelical church. By national church, I do not mean a denomination but the informal total of evangelical believers in the United States. Most evangelicals would say these folks are the true church of Christ's followers in the United States, or at least the bulk of it, based on our understanding of the New Testament.

We're talking about churches and individuals who believe a salvation-by-faith-alone "gospel." We're talking about American Christians who believe the Bible is God's Word, that it is without error, and that Jesus is the only way to salvation and to God. This broad group includes a wide variety: Pentecostals, Baptists, charismatics, fundamentalists, those who believe you can lose your salvation, those who believe you can't, Calvinistic, non-Calvinistic, and so forth. But all of these churches believe Jesus is the only way to God, and that Scripture is God's authoritative Word.

Some books assessing the United States church wander from "Protestants" (a huge category that includes millions who don't often believe Jesus is the only way or that the Bible is without error) to "born agains" (millions more who claim to be "born again" but don't exhibit any measurable difference from other Americans in religious activity) to "evangelicals" (the group that this book addresses). Mixing these labels can result in a lot of confusion and misunderstanding, because these groups are radically different in their sizes and habits.

Of course, evangelicals also report being born again, which adds to the confusion. But many Americans who self-report as "born again" are not actually evangelical Christians. We know this because we've seen study after study finding that many born agains believe that Allah is the same God as Jesus and other shocking findings. Clearly, the "born again" group is not equal to the evangelical group (though it overlaps with it). For the sake of focus, accuracy, and consistency, we're only examining evangelicals in our research. For a fuller definition of "evangelical," see appendix C.

I should warn you now that it's not easy wrapping our arms around the size of the evangelical church in the United States. This chapter's findings are challenging, and you may find yourself thinking, *That can't be right*. If your gut disagrees with the facts, keep this in mind. Your gut, like mine, is probably the gut of an ingrown evangelical. Many of us live in subcultural evangelical worlds. Everywhere we look we see believers—at home, in our social circles, possibly even at work. We read and listen to media that are primarily evangelical. Our Facebook newsfeeds are clogged with other evangelicals, as are our podcasts, our bookshelves, and our calendars.

Our most strategic leaders are further insulated, spending their days in evangelical institutions. And many of our national leaders are triple insulated, living in evangelically saturated areas like Grand Rapids, Colorado Springs, Texas, and Bible-Belt metropolises.

Michael Hyatt, a 21st-century thinker and Christian publishing executive, put it well when he observed, "The problem is that insiders are often the ones least capable of seeing things from an outside perspective. It's difficult to get outside of our own paradigms. But it's imperative if our industry is going to be ready for the brave new world."[4] Hyatt is right. Groupthink and overexposure to our own movement can blind us to the reality of how we fit into the larger, rapidly changing culture.

So, with such an awareness of our own limitations, let us pull off the wrappings and answer the question, Just how big is the evangelical church in the United States?

Maybe you've heard that 70 to 80 percent of Americans are Christian. Or, chances are, you've heard the claim that 40 percent of Americans are born again. Many evangelicals assume we are a supermajority in the United States, because we've heard these figures recycled and recited by leaders we trust.

But could it really be that if you took a random sampling of ten Americans from movie theaters and Walmarts between New York and Los Angeles, eight would be Bible-believing evangelical Christians? Does it seem realistic that four of the ten, or two in every five Americans, would be evangelicals?

Nope. You don't have to talk, work, or study outside evangelical circles for long to realize that we are not possibly that much of the United States population in the 21st century. No matter how you stack it, evangelicals do not account for eight in every ten Americans. We don't account for four in ten either. At best, according to the most optimistic reports, we are two in every ten Americans. And now, a consensus of the most dedicated researchers pins the number at *less than* one in ten.

By multiple accounts, evangelical believers are between 7 and 9 percent of the United States population.

If these findings are correct (and they've been confirmed by a handful of separate researchers), then the actual number of evangelicals in the United States is not the 128 million we've been told.[5] No, of America's 316 million residents, we evangelicals only account for about 22 to 28 million. As mentioned before, we lose about 2.6 million of those each decade. And the number of our new converts does not hold our position with population growth.

In the next decades we will see a massive decrease in evangelical influence politically, economically, culturally, and financially. Ministry managers at the leading edge of evangelicalism already sense these losses. Of two thousand United States church leaders recently surveyed, some 82 percent said that we are already losing influence as a movement.[6] Around the world, no other church leaders from any other continent or country reported such a loss of influence in their home country.

- We are losing influence because we are shrinking.
- We are losing influence because the host culture is changing so much faster than we (or even it) can understand.
- We are losing influence because the United States population is booming faster than it was during the Baby Boom, and our movement is not keeping up with the growth.
- We are also losing influence because culture at large is realizing, formally or informally, that evangelicals are not as big or significant as we have claimed. Whether by percent of population, power of vote, or simple cultural influence, we are no longer as mighty as we once were.

Our naïve overestimation shows in embarrassing ways. Take for example the fruitless eight-year evangelical boycott of Disney. Together, the Southern Baptists and other evangelical groups claimed that tens of millions of evangelicals would stop buying Disney products. The culture at large and Disney shareholders watched the company's profits and stock value nearly double during the boycott years.

If the boycott proved anything, it proved that we evangelicals overestimate our size and influence as a movement. This point was further emphasized when the leaders who withdrew the boycott warned Disney that they would be keeping an eye on them.[7]

Just as housing values plummeted with the "burst real estate bubble" of the financial recession, evangelical influence will plummet during the Great Evangelical Recession. The broad-shouldered claims and threats of evangelical leaders will be increasingly comical and laughable to outsiders in the know.

The realization that homes weren't worth nearly their sales prices was one factor in a larger economic recession. The dawning realization that evangelicalism is smaller than she has claimed will be a triggering factor in the Great Evangelical Recession of the next decades.

When society at large understands that evangelicals are no longer the juggernaut we claimed to be in the 1980s and 1990s, there will be repercussions. Here's how one outsider, a religion journalist, put it when she realized the actual size of evangelicalism in the United States:

A small and declining group of people has been portrayed as tremendously powerful and growing so rapidly that they might take over the country—when in fact the number of converts among this group is down and dropping. They are rarely able to convert an adult, middle-class American. Their share of the population is not 25 percent, but at most 7 percent of the country and falling. All these numbers come from the churches themselves.[8]

Separately, evangelical researchers Thom and Sam Rainer concluded, "Most churches are dwindling. Most denominations are not growing. The population in the United States is exploding . . . the church is losing ground. We are in a steep state of decline."[9]

Independent Experts Conclude Evangelicalism Is About One-Fourth the Size Often Claimed

So why do we commonly hear that we're a larger movement? Well, for starters, it's easy to misinterpret numbers. Also, high figures are tossed about with well-intentioned ignorance, because we do not understand that "Christians," "Protestants," "born agains," and "evangelicals" are radically different groups.

Here's the sort of technically accurate but confusing statistic we often hear. In the 2009 American Religious Identification Survey, 76 percent of Americans self-identified as "Christian."[10] If we're not careful, we might think the majority of the country understands Christ, the Bible, and Christianity the way we evangelicals do. Unfortunately, that's not the case.

Sociologists have long known that Americans who self-identify as "Christian" rarely attend any church, let alone an evangelical one. Of the minority who do attend church, large segments are Catholic, non-Bible-believing, non-Christ-believing, or even Mormon. In short, the vast majority are not Christians by the evangelical definition of trusting in Christ alone for eternal salvation and valuing God's Word as the true standard for belief and practice.

This is why Gallup asks respondents if they are "born again." Gallup surveys indicate that perhaps one-third, possibly as high as 45 percent, of Americans claim to be born again.[11] That would be almost one-in-two Americans.

For a long time, influential evangelicals assumed that the folks who claimed to be born again were all evangelicals. This figure is the reason why we often hear that about 40 percent of Americans are evangelical Christians. But specialists have learned recently that, as with the term "Christian," the term "born again" means different things to different people in postmodern, pluralistic America.

We're going to see a massive discrepancy between the number of Americans who claim to be born again and the experts' count of evangelicals. The reason for the discrepancy is simple: A lot of Americans *say* they're born again, but when prodded, they do not believe what evangelical Christians believe.[12]

For this reason, a growing host of sociologists, journalists, and academics believe that the "born again" figure does not represent the actual count of evangelical Christians, any more than the "Christian" figure does.

Let's now look at four nationally recognized specialists, each with differing credentials, differing motivations, and differing research methodologies. To protect the flow of thought, I won't dissect their research strategies here. However, these experts explain their methodologies in their footnoted works.

Separately, all four researchers have found that evangelicals account for 7 to 8.9 percent of the United States population. That is, not even one in ten Americans.

Dr. Christian Smith, Professor of Sociology at Notre Dame: Evangelicals Are 7 Percent of the United States

Respected sociologist Dr. Christian Smith employed academically rigorous methodology to reach his conclusion that about 20 million Americans "identify themselves with the evangelical movement."[13]

Dr. Smith is professor of sociology and director of the Center for the Study of Religion and Society at the University of Notre Dame. Not only is he a highly esteemed sociologist at a leading religious university, he is also a specialist in studying religious groups.

Dr. Smith is not a theologian or church leader giving an opinion on the size of evangelicalism. He is an uncontested and proven academic who undertook a formal survey. Smith's sociology education includes both a masters and PhD from Harvard. Smith is also a Christian, with no motivation to minimize the size of evangelicalism. According to Dr. Smith's rigorous sociological survey methods, we evangelicals make up about 7 percent of the United States population.

David T. Olson, American Church Research Project: Evangelicals Are 8.9 Percent of the United States

David T. Olson is a different kind of researcher—not an academic, but a specialist in the practical. He directs the American Church Research Project, which maintains a database of more than 200,000

United States churches. Like many academics, Olson thinks the "born again" question is a simplistic and flawed way of calculating belief.

Olson is among a growing number who don't trust Americans to understand the religious lingo in phone surveys or to be honest about their church attendance. Olson and a handful of sociologists have proven that Americans round up and outright inflate their answers about church attendance, Bible reading, and other religious activities. For Olson, actions speak louder than words. He writes:

> The Gallup Organization reports that more than 40 percent of Americans say that in the last week they attended a house of worship. . . . If these poll numbers reflected reality, between 120 and 129 million Americans should be in a worship service on any given weekend. However, these numbers do not reflect reality. When you start to do the math, the vision of a booming American church unravels. . . .
>
> In reality the church in America is not booming. It is in crisis. On any given Sunday, the vast majority of Americans are absent from church. Even more troublesome, as the American population continues to grow, the church falls further and further behind.[14]

Ultimately, Olson concludes that 8.9 percent of Americans attend evangelical church services.[15] And that may be slightly high, for the following reason.

Olson's numbers don't rely on individuals to self-report their church involvement, but they do rely on churches to self-report their attendance. As an evangelical "senior pastor," I've seen some churches round up or outright inflate their own numbers. If that's a widespread reality, then Olson's conclusion that 8.9 percent of Americans regularly attend evangelical churches may be slightly higher than reality.

It is exactly 1.9 percent higher than the Barna Group's recent finding.

Barna Group, Most Experienced Evangelical Pollsters: Evangelicals Are 7 Percent of the United States

The Barna Group has been tracking the evangelical church for about three decades. They are probably the most sophisticated and experienced auditors of United States evangelicalism in the world.

In George Barna's 2011 book, *Futurecast*, he reports the findings of a Barna Group survey, which found that "about 7 percent of the public can be considered evangelical Christians." Barna's methodology is related to Gallup's—surveys of a statistically accurate sample group. But the Barna Group puts intentional thought into the wording of their questions. They work harder than anyone else to craft a custom net that will catch only evangelical Christians (while leaving great space for evangelical diversity including fundamentalists, charismatics, non-charismatics, and so forth).

Their figure of 7 percent is down from a 2007 Barna finding of 8 percent,[16] which was down about one-third from Barna's count in 1991. We should note that George Barna has received recent criticism for the fine net he casts to draw out only evangelicals. This criticism is often based on opinion, not data. The corroborating conclusions of the three other independent researchers identified here indicate that the Barna Group, which has been measuring exclusively evangelicals for decades now, does indeed know how to measure evangelicals.

From everything I can see, the Barna Group's figure, like the figures of the other experts here, is accurate. Let's not shoot the messenger.

Christine Wicker, Award-Winning Religion Reporter: Evangelicals Are 7 Percent of the United States

Christine Wicker, a mainstream journalist, is not an evangelical. As such, she brings a fresh objectivity to our national headcount. Wicker has spent years reporting on and measuring the size of the evangelical church. Her methods and motives differ from Smith's, Olson's, or Barna's. Her conclusion, however, is identical.

Wicker started with in-house numbers from the Southern Baptists—the largest organized group of evangelicals—to demonstrate how inflated our count is. The Southern Baptists reported their membership at 16 million Americans, but by their own records they only had about 6.1 million attending their services on any given Sunday in 2007, she found.[17]

In the years since Wicker's investigation, Southern Baptist leaders have publicly stated that the group is struggling. A 2011 report confirmed a continuing trend of decreasing attendance, membership, giving, and conversions among Southern Baptist churches. Ed Stetzer, president of the Southern Baptist research arm, LifeWay, put it this way: "This is not a blip. This is a trend. And the trend is one of decline."[18]

The Southern Baptists may be the best microcosm of evangelicalism in the United States. Their values and methods are largely in line with the broad mainstream movement. Where the majority of evangelicalism is scattered and difficult to track, the Southern Baptists do an excellent job tracking the trends in their large chunk of the national evangelical church.

And here's their recent trajectory. This largest group in evangelicalism, the group that produced Rick Warren and of which Saddleback remains a part, is not maintaining its size with population growth.

Wicker also examined the National Association of Evangelicals' claim to represent "thirty million" evangelicals. After adding up the total number of attendees in each of the sixty-one represented denominations and estimating the attendance of the other NAE churches, Wicker could only account for 7.6 million evangelicals represented by the NAE.[19] When she confronted the NAE with these findings, they did not refute her conclusion and removed the claim of representing thirty million evangelicals from their website, according to her book.

Wicker concluded that, using evangelical's own figures, about 7 percent of Americans are evangelicals. That's exactly the same as Barna's 2011 figure. It's within spitting distance of Olson's figure, and it's the same as the esteemed academic Dr. Christian Smith's.

Four specialized researchers. Four independent methods of thorough calculation. Four unique motivations. One conclusion: The actual number of evangelical Christians is far less than we've been told, accounting for 7 to 8.9 percent of the United States population, not 40 percent and certainly not 70 percent.

If you still doubt the experts' findings, examine their methodology for yourself. Or better yet, do a study in your own community.

Add up the average attendance at the evangelical churches in your neighborhood, city, or county. Then compare that figure to the neighborhood, city, or county's population. If you live in a typical community, the combined church attendance will account for 5 to 10 percent of the population. Some Bible Belt and Midwest areas will be higher. Most metropolitan areas will be much lower.

According to the specialists, the total number of evangelicals is about 22 million of America's 316 million residents, rather than the oft-touted figure of 128 million who claim to be born again, but don't actually understand what that means.[20] If the generational changes examined in the upcoming chapters persist, evangelicals could drop to about 4 percent of the population within three decades. That is, in just under thirty years, we may only be 16 million of about 400 million Americans.[21] That's one in every twenty-five Americans.

So, even as many outsiders in the host culture assume that we are a dominant and bigoted majority, Bible-believing evangelicals are becoming, almost overnight, a shrinking minority. In economic terms, it's a market correction—much like the plummeting home prices of the Great (financial) Recession.

Choosing Not to Ignore the Facts

> Maybe if I ignore the truth long enough, it won't be the truth. Maybe if you don't get the facts, the facts will just go away. . . . That approach never leads to anywhere good.
>
> Andy Stanley, in the sermon series DEFINING MOMENTS

Experts will continue debating and refining evangelicalism's size and definition. Already, some reputable observers have refuted the findings above, arguing that the true size of evangelicalism is closer to 20 percent. The point here is simply that, according to a growing host of specialists, our size is dramatically smaller than we have been told.

Even if we optimistically triple the 7 percent to 21 percent, the evangelical church is still half the size we've been told. The repercussions are massive. We are nowhere near half the country—as many have claimed. This is a huge drop in our size and influence.

In Romans 12:3, the apostle Paul tells Christ's followers, "For by the grace given me I say to every one of you: Do not think of yourself more highly than you ought, but rather think of yourself with sober judgment. . . ." Here God commands us to measure ourselves accurately—to *not* round up, to be honest.

Whether on purpose or by accident, some evangelicals have overstated the size of our movement. Many of us have repeated the figures, assuming them to be accurate. As with pre-recession home prices, we have seen and heard these figures so repeatedly that we cannot fathom the possibility of these numbers being wrong.

Our value has been inflated, and, like the bubble of home values, the market will correct. Our actual size will show itself. It's already beginning to—in national elections, television programming, and local school board decisions. After all, if anyone believes that the truth always wins out, it's us evangelicals.

As I have ricocheted between secular journalism and evangelical Christianity, I've noticed a trend in truth telling. Some of my agnostic journalism colleagues don't believe in absolute moral truth, but when it comes to reporting—even on their own flaws—they are a brutally accurate and honest bunch.

Conversely, we evangelicals build our entire system on a belief in "absolute truth." We read books about it. We teach absolute truth to our kids. And yet, we prophets of absolute truth sometimes help God out by rounding up—our weekly church attendance and, it seems, our national headcount, too.

If anyone, we should know that lying never pays. In fact, it almost always costs.

Evangelicals Are About the Population of New York State

In this chapter we have built a framework, so that we can interpret the trends in the rest of the book. Let's finish by visualizing our findings.

If you would, picture a map of this country's fifty states. Most of us have been told and have the impression that about half the country is evangelical. So you can imagine that on your United States map, half of the states are evangelical. You might even pick a color for the evangelical states and another color for the nonbelieving states. These "evangelical" states previously represented between 40 and 70 percent of the population, depending on which figure you had previously been told.

Now, we have seen that in reality, the population of evangelical Christians in the United States is much smaller. It's actually about the population of New York State, around 22 million. So now make New York State the "evangelical" color, and change every other state to the color of nonbelievers. Picture all forty-nine of the other states as nonbelieving. That's the reality of our size in the United States.

To put it in international terms, there are slightly more evangelicals in the entire United States than there are Muslims in the greater metro area of Cairo, Egypt.[22]

You could put it this way. If we asked New York State's 21 million residents to leave, then we could take every evangelical Christian in the United States, and take over New York State. Once all 22 million of us populated New York, there would not be a single evangelical Christian among the 294 million Americans remaining in the other forty-nine states.

This is our actual size, according to the researchers who specialize in counting evangelicals.

In future chapters, we'll see that our smaller size is slowly shrinking—because we're losing our own kids and we're failing to generate significant converts in the midst of a rapid population boom. But there's a more practical and immediate evangelical crisis on the horizon: a culture crisis.

2

Hated

Then a new king, who did not know about Joseph, came to power in Egypt.

Exodus 1:8

Initially I titled this book *The Sound of a Dying Church*. Towering, centuries-old trees don't make any sound when they begin dying. They appear to be in good health—until a tremor of snapping branches announces their collapse to the forest floor. While their deaths seem sudden, old trees actually endure a long, silent dying process.

The tree of evangelicalism in the United States is centuries old. She is a mighty oak with deep roots. So many saplings have grown up under her shade—trees of education, reform, freedom, invention, work ethic, resourcefulness, wealth, and science.

Two forces kill old strong trees: Internal diseases rot the trees from within, and external forces shake the trees from without. In the following chapters, we will see the diseases eating the oak of evangelicalism from within. She struggles with the rot of lost limbs and branches (Bleeding) and the inability to create new life and leaves (Sputtering). As a result, she is feebler and less powerful than she used to be (Inflated and Bankrupt). We'll also see that just as these diseases have set in, the oak of evangelicalism is splintering apart (Dividing), dividing herself over disputes.

In addition to these internal sicknesses, the oak of evangelicalism will face, in the next fifty years, a hurricane force wind of external change. Humanly speaking, the combination of these forces may be too much.

As the psalmist writes, "My salvation and my honor depend on God" (Psalm 62:7). God will prevail, but the oak of United States evangelical Christianity *as we know it* may not. She would not be the first mighty oak of Christianity to fall. She is quietly dying, internally. And now we see that, as she deteriorates internally, she also faces the external storms and pressures of a lifetime.

The coming storms of change are no accident. They are the planned and pained schemes of demonic manipulation—the endgame of a strategic enemy who has been plotting and machinating against the United States church for decades.[1]

In Tolkien's *The Two Towers*, a Satan-figure, the white-haired wizard Saruman, orders his demonic minions to uproot a grove of ancient trees. He burns them to create fuel for more evil. The warriors of darkness hack, tear, and tug at the ancient trees until they topple—until their roots rip out of the earth with a centuries-old groaning. We have heard the groaning of ancient Christian trees across the Atlantic. We have heard the echoes of their collapse. Now I believe we are seeing just such a demonic strain against the mature oak of evangelicalism in the United States.

The battle has been planned for lifetimes, but we're only now seeing the teeth of the struggle. We are seeing early signs that demonstrate the severity of a coming conflict. These recent headlines demonstrate how the "prince of this world" (John 12:31) is advancing deeper into the forest of the United States.

"California Pastor Arrested for Reading Bible in Public"—May 23, 2011, ChristianExaminer.com

"Christian Ministers Arrested for Praying Near Gay Festival"— July 10, 2007, FreeRepublic.com

"Christians Arrested for Proselytizing Near Muslim Gathering in Dearborn Michigan"—June 19, 2010, Politics4all.com

"Pastor Is Shot and Killed at Illinois Church"—March 8, 2009, *New York Times*

"Shooting at the Family Research Council: Hate from the Left"—August 17, 2012, *Washington Times*

"Gay Fascists Storm Church, Attack Members"—November 13, 2008, Onenewsnow.com

"California University [policy handbook] Defines Christians as Oppressors"—February 16, 2011, FoxNews.com

"Burritos OK, Bible Not, in Oklahoma School District"—October 30, 2011, *Washington Examiner*

"Oklahoma Police Captain Faces Disciplinary Action for Refusing to Attend [mandatory] Islamic Event"—February 23, 2011, FoxNews.com

"Texas School Punishes Boy for Opposing Homosexuality"—September 22, 2011, FoxNews.com

Each headline, from various corners of the United States, has a backstory. I'd like to tell you the common theme behind two other stories. They are separate stories, from separate states, but oddly similar.

In April of 2008 Crystal Dixon, a human relations administrator at the University of Toledo, wrote a letter to the editor of her local newspaper.

Earlier, the editor of the local paper had compared the homosexual struggle to the race struggle of the Civil Rights era. Dixon, an African-American and an evangelical, wrote to say that she didn't think being born black and being gay were the same. She explained her view on homosexuality as a choice and clarified that "human beings, regardless of their choices in life, are of ultimate value to God and should be viewed the same by others."[2]

Dixon wrote the letter on her own time, and she didn't refer to her position at the university. Still, university officials fired her three days after her letter was printed. They clarified that her letter was the reason for the termination. Other university employees had openly taken pro-homosexual views in local newspapers, without consequence.[3] But Dixon was terminated for expressing her Christian belief—not for calling gays terrible names, but for suggesting, outside of university circles, that she believes homosexuals have a choice in their sexual orientation.

Dixon's story is similar to another. Julea Ward is also an evangelical. Like Dixon, she also happens to be African-American and a woman—not your stereotypical picture of a bigoted white male Protestant.

Ward was studying counseling at Eastern Michigan University when she learned a client of hers was homosexual. Rather than tell a nonbelieving counseling client that homosexuality is wrong, as she believes, Ward tried to do the professional thing. She saw a potential conflict of interest, so she asked her supervisor what she should do.

Ward's professors eventually explained that she would have to attend a remediation program. She would not be allowed to counsel anyone until she could "see the error of her ways" and change her beliefs about homosexuality.

When Ward explained that she did not want to offend anyone, but that she would not be changing her beliefs, the faculty expelled her from the counseling program, because of her biblical beliefs.

The recent Chick-fil-A saga is another example of the growing prejudice against evangelicals. Ten years ago, could anyone have imagined the mayors of cities like New York and Boston attempting to expel a national chain from their cities, simply because of the owner's private religious beliefs? Weeks later, a shooting at the Family Research Council's headquarters further demonstrated this when an LGBT activist carrying Chick-fil-A sandwiches and a gun shot a security guard in the conservative Christian organization's lobby.

The sum of the evidence is clear. Internal forces are already weakening the tree of evangelicalism in the United States, but in coming decades United States evangelicals will be tested as never before, by the ripping and tearing of external cultural change—a force more violent than many of us expect.

Evangelicalism in the United States has stood strong through centuries of difficulties and setbacks. She has not seen anything quite like what she will see in the next fifty years.

It's easy to sensationalize a coming "persecution" against Bible-believing Christians in the United States. That's not my aim here. I'm not suggesting that we'll see Soviet-style Gulags or Nazi-style death camps on United States soil.

Here's what I am suggesting:

1. The broader "host" culture of the United States is changing faster than most of us realize.
2. The direction of that change includes pro-homosexuality and anti-Christian reactionism.
3. The rate of the cultural change in this direction will further accelerate as the oldest two generations die, taking their traditional "American values" and votes with them.
4. These changes will reach a point at which they directly affect church as we know it and our lives as individual evangelicals.

Already, in the firing and expulsion of the two evangelicals above, we see that these trends are in play. United States culture is quickly reshaping itself. As Billy Graham recently wrote in the foreword of his updated book *Storm Warning*, "Now at ninety-one years old, I believe the storm clouds are darker than they have ever been. The world has changed dramatically."

1. The "host" culture is changing faster than most of us (inside and out of the church) realize.

The United States has shifted into a postmodern and post-Christian age. Nobody contests this. The real question is, How fast is culture in the United States changing? How long until changing beliefs reshape legislation, institutions, and cultural norms in America?

Well, we can't say for sure. Measuring the speed of cultural change is like catching a blue whale with your bare hands. Predicting how culture will change is even more precarious.

As the speed of cultural change has notably accelerated, a handful of observers have become specialists in attempting to measure its rate of change. Known as futurists, these mathematical prophets combine statistics, sociology, psychology, and intuition to chart changes in culture and tentatively predict the future. Most futurists are secular agnostics, but many evangelical observers agree with them on this: Around the globe, cultures are changing faster than ever before in human history, mostly because we are communicating and processing information exponentially faster.

When more than a hundred leading secular futurists were surveyed, the common shared view about our present culture was, "We are in the midst of a historical transformation. Current times are just not part of normal history."[4]

In other words, culture is changing faster than it typically has in world history. Ten years from now it will be changing even faster, due to accelerating technology advancements. As a result, it is impossible to anticipate just how quickly United States culture will quake and reshape during our lifetimes.

In *Futurecast*, George Barna writes, "America is undergoing significant changes, and the nature of those changes is both complex and chaotic. The historical foundations on which our society was developed are facing some severe challenges. It's not easy to be the kind of Christian that Jesus longs to have as His ambassadors in this place, at this time."[5]

This accelerating rate of cultural change is not limited to the United States. The toppling of governments in Libya and Egypt during the Arab Spring of 2011 are two demonstrations of technology's role in accelerating cultural change. Consider that for thousands of years Egyptians have never once been able to overthrow a ruler. In 2011, we saw them use Twitter, a technology less than six years old, to oust a ruler who had been untouchable for decades. In a historic view, the abruptness of this change is mind-blowing.

Months after the Arab Spring, London and surrounding cities saw their own unexpected riots and temporary mob anarchy. One British journalist remarked:

> The speed of the disintegration said everything. It took less than 48 hours for London to descend from self-styled capital of the world into a circuit of burning dystopian hells. The speed of BlackBerry messaging; the speed of kids on BMXs; the speed of Molotovs and petrol. Never mind the police, even the media couldn't keep up.[6]

Futurist Ray Kurzweil explained the rate of change this way:

> Our forebears expected the future to be pretty much like their present, which had been pretty much like their past. . . . But the future will be far more surprising than most observers realize: few have truly internalized the implications of the fact that the rate of change itself is accelerating.[7]

He adds:

> An analysis of the history of technology shows that technological change is exponential. . . . So we won't experience 100 years of progress in the 21st century—it will be more like 20,000 years of progress (at today's rate).[8]

If you're curious, you can research the science behind the "Law of Accelerated Returns" or mathematician Vernor Vinge's views on "accelerating change." The bottom line is that the speed of cultural change in the United States is accelerating. And it continues to accelerate.

This fact alone is not good or bad news. It's just a fact. And it means that, barring some miraculous revival, the culture will continue on its current course—gaining speed in the direction it's already heading.

New technology does not change a culture's direction. It simply accelerates the change. For example, the new technology of the printing press did not change the direction of culture during the Reformation. Rather, the new technology ignited the Protestant breakthroughs that had already been building pressure in the "Christian" culture of the 1400s and 1500s. Most recently, the mobile Internet has broken loose movements that have been building for decades in the Middle and Near East.

Let's now examine the established direction of change in United States culture. This direction was in place as the Internet came to life. It was further cemented into place during the personal and portable web revolution of 2000 to 2010, and it is now undeniably the course and direction of accelerating change in the United States.

2. The direction of accelerating change includes anti-Christian reactionism and pro-homosexuality.

The hurtling rocket of cultural change in the United States includes dozens of trajectories. Dr. David Jeremiah documents some of these abrupt culture shifts in his book *I Never Thought I'd See the Day! Culture at the Crossroads.* Dr. Jeremiah writes that he never expected to see the day

"When Atheists Would Be Angry,"
"When Christians Wouldn't Know They Were in a War,"
"When Morality Would Be in a Free Fall,"
"When the Bible Would Be Marginalized," and
"When the Church Would Be Irrelevant."[9]

Dr. Jeremiah comments:

Something has happened in America that once seemed unthinkable to me. When I was a boy growing up and even a young man in school, biblical principles had a strong influence in society. I don't mean everyone was religious, or even that religion was dominant in everyone's thinking. Yet there was a pervasive respect for the Bible, and biblical principles were evident in the shape of the culture and the mores of the people. It never occurred to me that the Bible could be marginalized and even vilified publicly as it is today.[10]

In 1984, just before his death, Francis Schaeffer rightly identified the direction of American cultural change.

> The world spirit of our age rolls on and on claiming to be autonomous and crushing all that we cherish in its path. Sixty years ago could we have imagined that unborn children would be killed by the millions here in our own country? Or that we would have *no freedom of speech* when it comes to speaking of God and biblical truth in our public schools? Or that every form of sexual perversion would be promoted by the entertainment media? Or that marriage, raising children, and family life would be objects of attack?[11]

Schaeffer wrote that the United States was undergoing a culture shift—in the same trajectory as post-Christian Europe: "Having turned away from the knowledge given by God, the Christian influence on the whole of culture has been lost. . . . Ours is a post-Christian world."[12]

Schaeffer's predictions about the continued decline of American culture have proved accurate. What would Schaeffer think, conclude, and predict if he could see what we're seeing today? His prophetic writing was, in many ways, ahead of its time. Now, even Schaeffer's long view seems too short to capture the rate of change in the 21st century.

As Dr. Jeremiah and Francis Schaeffer both suggest, many of the culture's changing trajectories directly affect the evangelical church. We will focus on two. Future America of 2020 to 2050 will be

- increasingly anti-Bible-believer
- increasingly pro-homosexual

Future America Is Reactionary Against Bible-Believing Christianity

In 2011, George Barna found that "people are more likely than not to acknowledge that Americans are becoming more hostile and negative toward Christianity."[13]

Secular sociologists have also noticed a reactive antagonism against Christians. Younger Americans increasingly resent Bible-believing Christianity. The culture is not just apathetically drifting from Christianity, as it did in the late 20th century. Now its leading edges are violently reacting to the grip that conservative Christianity and the religious right held for so many decades.

We will see this in population demographics in chapter 6 (Sputtering), which documents the church's failure to convert non-believing Americans. Americans under the age of thirty-five are four times more likely to be atheistic, agnostic, or nonreligious. Their secular worldview affects the greater United States culture and, in coming decades, will reshape federal, state, and local governments, as well as less formal cultural norms.

In 2007, the *Atlantic* reported that Berkley sociologists had documented a sudden and radical antagonism toward organized Christianity, particularly among younger Americans.[14]

The reaction against conservative Christians continues to accelerate. In his book *Bad Religion*, Ross Douthat writes, "In a 2002 paper in the *American Sociological Review*, [researchers] announced the startling fact that the percentage of Americans who said they had 'no religious preference' had doubled in less than ten years. . . ." By the late 2000s that same number had quadrupled.[15]

Right now, evangelicals account for a minority of the United States population. But a giant chunk of Americans, most people over the age of fifty-five, still see life through a quasi-Christian lens. They are the non-evangelicals who grew up in the Sunday schools of the 1940s to early '60s. Even if their parents weren't some sort of Christian, their friends or neighbors or teachers were. They still had prayer in their schools. Intentionally or not, they are the dam holding traditional American values in place.

In the next ten to thirty years, as the oldest two generations pass off the scene, the tides of the new American worldview will push through this decades-old barrier, radically redefining United States culture. As these generations pass away, opposition and antagonism against evangelicals will continue to be a natural result, according to Harvard economists:

Religion stirs up the most controversy. . . . The more evenly divided a culture finds itself on the ultimate questions, the more likely politicians are to pursue "strategic extremism" and mobilize one side against the other. Precisely this kind of polarization dominated European politics from the French Revolution until the middle of the 20th century, sparking regular clashes—Germany's Kulturkampf, France's Dreyfuss Affair, Spain's Civil War—between secular and religious ideologies.[16]

Indeed, Americans are currently polarized on the "ultimate questions" of our day. From same-sex marriage to size of government, abortion, and even presidential elections, more and more polls are landing at near 50-50 splits. As a result, we are seeing the intense controversy that the Harvard economists describe as historically common. Resulting from that controversy is the antagonism against "Christians" and the religious right. Unfortunately for evangelicals, the majority of "Christian" and "conservative" Americans will die off in the next thirty years—even as the angst against conservative Christians continues to gain momentum.

The end result will eventually be a culture where the majority of Americans has an enemy view of Bible-believing Christians, while the evangelical movement shrinks into further minority status.

What does American antagonism against Christians look like? We see it foreshadowed today in various corners of United States culture.

In business, Google, the most powerful 21st-century web and communications company, recently unveiled a powerful package of online tools for nonprofit organizations. The package normally costs thousands of dollars, but qualifying nonprofits could use the web tools for free, as Google's donation to society. However, the following groups did not qualify as nonprofits: "churches, proselytizing groups, and any organization that considers religion or sexual orientation in hiring decisions."[17] Churches were not accidentally excluded from the program, but intentionally so. Google's policy was reversed shortly before this book was printed, but it was a signpost of a culture that is radically different from the United States culture of the 20th century.

The power brokers in the new United States are unaware of the positive role that Christianity once played in the nation. It is reminiscent of the passage in Exodus 1:8, describing why a new Pharaoh enslaved the Hebrews: "Then a new king, who did not know about Joseph, came to power in Egypt."

We see many more signposts of cultural direction in academics. One professor and social worker from Arizona State University, Dr. David Hodges, suggests that the present academic system is inadvertently training "prejudice against Evangelicals" into social workers. His conclusion, as an insider, aligns with a lot of other data.

Prejudice against Bible-believing Christians is not a future thing. It is a present cultural direction that will amplify in the coming decades.

In 2011, *The Chronicle of Higher Education* reported that in a formal survey, American sociologists said they would be "less likely to hire" a job candidate who is evangelical. Of the sociologists interviewed, 39.1 percent overtly said they would discriminate against a job candidate who is evangelical. These are the experts who measure and manage cultural change. Nearly half of them outright admit prejudice against evangelicals.[18]

Can you imagine a sociologist outright saying they would be less likely to hire a homosexual or a Muslim?

Why is prejudice against evangelicals accepted? It may be because we have convinced so many outsiders that we are so much larger and more powerful than we actually are, as explained in chapter 1.

The prejudice is not limited to sociologists. Martin Gaskell, an esteemed astronomer, lost his job offer at the University of Kentucky after a board member learned he was, as she wrote, "potentially evangelical."[19]

In fact, in the minds of American college and university professors, Muslims are a more peaceful and preferred people than evangelicals. Ten years after the terrorist attacks on the World Trade Center, and as Islamic extremists continue bombings and shootings around the world, the teachers of our children's teachers view Islam more favorably than they view evangelical Christianity.

A study by the non-evangelical group Jewish and Community Research asked 1,200 college and university professors if they had "unfavorable feelings" toward various religions.[20]

Less than one in four college and university professors have negative feelings toward Muslims, but a majority of them have negative feelings toward evangelical Christians.

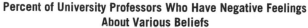

Percent of University Professors Who Have Negative Feelings About Various Beliefs

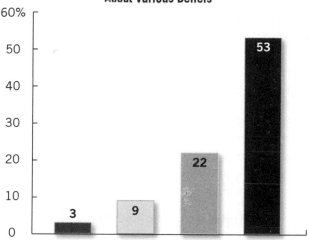

3% held unfavorable feelings for Jews.
9% held unfavorable feelings for non-evangelical Christians.
22% held unfavorable feelings for Muslims.
53% held unfavorable feelings toward evangelical Christians.

Of course, this isn't news for the evangelical college students who retain their faith during their college years. It's certainly not news for Emily Brooker. A student at Missouri State University, Brooker sat accused and embarrassed before a faculty panel as they charged her with discrimination against gays. Brooker's crime: She refused to sign and mail a letter supporting gay adoptions to a state legislator. The letter supporting gay adoption had been a required class assignment. Brooker was the only student who asked not to send the letter, which was required to be pro-gay adoption. The result: a public hearing in which faculty members accused her of discrimination.[21]

This prejudice against Bible-believing Christians will continue accelerating as it seeps from professors to impressionable students and then into the mainstream culture during the coming decades.

History has taught us, from Cambridge and Oxford in England to Harvard and Princeton in the early United States, that the mainstream thought in the university becomes, in time, the mainstream thought in the broader culture.

Future America of 2020–2050 Is Aggressively Pro-Homosexual

Evangelical observer Ed Stetzer was right when he wrote, "The issue of homosexuality will need to be increasingly addressed—and addressed graciously—in the Christian community."[22]

America's changing views on homosexuality are clear. Evangelicals are on a crash course with a tectonic culture shift that could categorize peaceful Bible-believing Christians with the Ku Klux Klan and abusive male chauvinists. If you think that sounds like an exaggeration, keep reading.

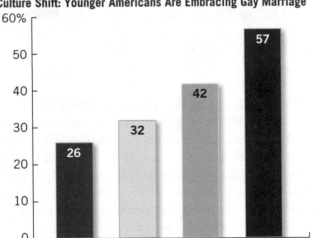

Culture Shift: Younger Americans Are Embracing Gay Marriage

26% of Americans age 65 and older favor gay marriage.
32% of Americans ages 50 to 64 favor gay marriage.
42% of Americans ages 30 to 49 favor gay marriage.
57% of Americans ages 18 to 29 favor gay marriage.

First, let's note how quickly United States culture is changing in its embrace of homosexuality. A 2011 survey by the Public Religion

Research Institute asked if participants favor same-sex marriage. Note the generational increase by age in the preceding chart.

Additionally, another 19 percent of 18- to 29-year-olds favor civil unions. In total, 76 percent of 18- to 29-year-olds favor some government-recognized union for homosexuals—as opposed to 26 percent among the oldest generation.[23]

Such generational trends tell the trajectory of the next fifteen years. Imagine the oldest generation disappearing off the above chart, and the new youngest generation following the patterned increase of percentage by generation, likely around 70 or 75 percent in favor. Fifteen more years pass, and the second oldest generation also disappears, replaced by a new young generation that is 85 to 95 percent in favor.

Future change aside, the last fifteen years demonstrate how quickly the United States culture is presently embracing homosexual marriage. Identical Gallup polls show the change. In 1996, some 68 percent of Americans opposed gay marriage, while only 27 percent favored it. By 2011, the numbers dramatically flipped, with a majority of 53 percent favoring gay marriage and only 45 percent opposing it.[24]

Do you think marriages between same-sex couples should or should not be recognized by the law as valid, with the same rights as traditional marriages?

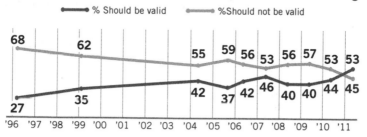

Note: Trend shown for polls in which same-sex marriage question followed questions on gay/lesbian rights and relations.
1996–2005 wording: "Do you think marriages between homosexuals . . ."

GALLUP

In the last fifteen years, the entire culture has flipped—on an issue that was basic and uncontested in the United States for 230 years. Fifteen years from now, an even smaller minority of

Americans will oppose gay marriage or civil unions. Thirty years from now, it may be as settled a matter as racial segregation—an issue that the culture is increasingly binding together as a direct parallel to homosexual rights.

What's happening isn't an isolated anomaly. It's the outgrowth of the new American worldview. Included in that worldview is the assumption that homosexuality is not a choice, and that it's a right to be protected just as race and gender should be. From this assumption, evangelicals are logically seen as the racists of the 21st century—opposing homosexual individuals and their rights.

For their book *unChristian*, researchers David Kinnaman and Gabe Lyons spent three years interviewing young Americans. They were surprised to learn that the most common belief about Bible-believing Christians today is that we are homophobic, anti-gay bigots. As Kinnaman and Lyons put it:

> The severity of the perception surprised me. . . . Out of twenty attributes that we assessed, both positive and negative, as they related to Christianity, the perception of being antihomosexual was at the top of the list. More than nine out of ten Mosaic and Buster outsiders (91 percent) said "antihomosexual" accurately describes present-day Christianity. . . .[25]
>
> In our research, the perception that Christians are "against" gays and lesbians—not only objecting to their lifestyles but also harboring irrational fear and unmerited scorn toward them—has reached critical mass. The gay issue has become the "big one," the negative image most likely to be intertwined with Christianity's reputation . . . surfacing a spate of negative perceptions: judgmental, bigoted, sheltered, right-wingers, hypocritical, insincere, and uncaring. Outsiders say our hostility toward gays—not just opposition to homosexual politics and behaviors but disdain for gay individuals—has become virtually synonymous with Christian faith.[26]

In the common worldview of Americans under forty, the evangelical understanding of homosexuality is hateful, small-minded, backward, and extremist. The stuff of cavemen and racists.

Abrupt cultural change also shows in how the American Psychiatric Association (APA) defines *homosexual*. The APA's *Diagnostic and Statistical Manual of Mental Disorders* (the DSM) defined homosexuality as a mental illness from its first printing in 1952 until 1973.[27]

In 1973 a small group of influential activists engineered the change in definition. You can listen to a fascinating Corporation for Public Broadcasting story about their mission to change the definition, footnoted here.[28]

I'm not suggesting that homosexuality is a mental illness. My point is that in the forty years since that change, homosexuality has evolved from illness to controversial, to exciting, to acceptable, and, within the last ten years, to a protected minority as fragile and important as being female or being African-American. Now, increasingly, anyone who is not an "ally" and fighting alongside the LGBT community is seen as a hateful bigot.

That's a radical change of cultural landscape in just four decades. This is the direction of the accelerating cultural change in the United States.

As of 2007, the same APA that once defined homosexuality as a mental illness says that a counselor who tries to change a gay client's sexual orientation may be harming the client.[29]

Evangelical counseling students are encountering expulsion and "remediation" across the country, even when they attempt to handle their difference of belief with integrity by self-identifying conflicts of interest.

It sounds sensational, but might it be, four decades from now, that the DSM includes a new mental illness—homophobia? That sounds like conjecture, right? I thought so, until I stumbled on a 2003 article in the *American Journal of Orthopsychiatry*. The journal article suggests that racism, sexism, and homophobia all be formally classified in one new DSM category as "intolerant personality disorder."[30]

Writing to their colleagues who determine DSM categories, psychologists did not recommend separate diagnoses for racism, sexism, or homophobia, but one single diagnosis. In other words, those who believe that homosexuality is a sin would be diagnosed with the same mental illness as a Ku Klux Klan racist. The article abstract explains:

Racism, sexism, and homophobia do not fit into any current diagnostic category. The authors propose that those who engage in
such behaviors display a form of psychopathology deserving of its
own category. The common denominator seems to be intolerance.
The authors explore the possibility of an intolerant personality
disorder, outline likely symptoms, and suggest some possible treatment considerations.[31]

Such is the possible post–baby boomer United States of 2030.
A person need not act out against homosexuals to have "intolerant personality disorder." Simply believing that homosexuality
is wrong puts you in the same blanket category as a racist or a
sexist—even if that moral belief never results in harmful behavior.

The European Union has already defined anyone with an "aversion" to homosexuality as homophobic, regardless of behavior or
speech. This is the definition from the January 2006 EU Resolution defining homophobia as a crime: "Homophobia can be defined as an irrational fear of and aversion to homosexuality and
to lesbian, gay, bisexual and transgender (LGBT) people based on
prejudice and similar to racism, xenophobia, anti-Semitism and
sexism. . . ."[32]

The resolution clarifies that the crime of homophobia is "often
hidden behind justifications based on . . . religious freedom and
the right to conscientious objection. . . ." Such religiously motivated "homophobia" is already viewed as equally heinous as racism. According to the resolution it is to be treated with "criminal
penalties."[33]

Of course, I believe—and every evangelical I respect believes—
that homosexual men or women should have the same basic human
rights and protections that all humans deserve. God calls us to
love homosexuals extravagantly, openly, and generously. Every
homosexual is loved by God and has eternal value, regardless of
what the culture calls "sexual orientation." As Christ's followers,
we are to show God's unconditional love to all humans, including
the most active in the gay community.

Our government should prosecute actual criminals who wrong
homosexuals, just as it would prosecute crimes against anyone else.

What I'm suggesting is the possibility that during the 21st century it may become a crime, a mental illness, or a "psychopathology" to simply believe that homosexuality is a sin.

If homophobia or "intolerant personality disorder" were to become diagnosable mental illnesses, how long would it take for Child Protective Services to begin removing children from homes where parents exhibit the mental illness of homophobia? Constitutional protections for freedom of religion do not typically apply to the mentally ill.

Homophobia as a mental illness may sound farfetched to you. I agree that it's impossible to predict the future diagnoses of the DSM. The point is simply that the worldview of future Americans is increasingly one that sees disagreement with a homosexual lifestyle as prejudiced, bigoted, dangerous, and hateful. We are already seeing such a worldview in many halls of influence and power.

As if to prove this point, the governor of California recently signed bill SB1172 into law, which makes it illegal for any counselor or family therapist in California to counsel minors away from homosexual sex. If a teen's parent desires counseling—or the teen himself or herself desires help—it is still illegal to discourage homosexual impulses. The law makes no exceptions for any religious beliefs or Christian counselors.[34] The mere fact that such a law could make it to a governor's desk in today's political climate foreshadows the challenges that lie ahead as the culture continues racing in this direction.

Ed Stetzer has rightly observed, "The culture sees this as a 'justice' issue—Christians discriminating on the basis of immutable characteristics."[35]

Less sensational are the underlying assumptions demonstrated in more and more contemporary news stories. Take for example a July 16, 2011, New York Times article. It's one of hundreds of contemporary artifacts that demonstrate how Bible-believing Christians are increasingly perceived as bigots. (Some accuse such newspaper reporters of inserting intentional bias, by *portraying* evangelicals this way. As a mainstream journalist, I would suggest that these reporters honestly *perceive* reality this way themselves, because of the assumptions and rules of our rapidly changing culture.)

In the story, politician Michele Bachmann is guilty by association because her husband, a Christian counselor, *may have possibly* given Christian counsel to a gay man who asked for help. An undercover homosexual investigator covertly recorded counseling sessions, and the reporter bandied the recordings as investigative reporting—even though no single quote was incriminating enough to print in the article.

Here's one paragraph from the piece:

> Questions about whether Dr. Bachmann offers reparative, or conversion, therapy have been percolating for years, fueled partly by his friendship with Janet Boynes, a Minneapolis minister who says she was "called out of homosexuality" by God, and partly by his argument that children are at risk when parents and educators tolerate homosexuality.[36]

To understand the Bible literally, to believe that homosexual sex is a sin, is political and career suicide in 21st-century America.

President Obama seems aware of the anti-Christian, pro-homosexual cultural tides. His White House has been the first in years to not participate in the National Day of Prayer and celebrate homosexuality instead.

On May 5, 2011, the National Day of Prayer passed without fanfare at the White House. There were no preachers or rabbis or public prayers of any sort. But later that month, there was plenty of fanfare. On May 31, 2011, the president of the United States issued a presidential proclamation, reminding Americans that June is "Lesbian, Gay, Bisexual, and Transgender Pride Month."

Where the 236-year-old tradition of prayer was once celebrated, the president now hosted parties and receptions for national leaders whose movement is not only about homosexuality, but also about the right to have sex with both men and women as a bisexual. This is an American freedom to be not just protected, but celebrated in the 21st-century United States. The president was not just accepting or listening to the movement but pressing its agenda on the nation, with fanfare.

The Federal government website Whitehouse.gov/LGBT documents the White House partnership with the LGBT movement.

At one White House celebration during Lesbian, Gay, Bisexual, and Transgender Pride Month, President Obama summarized the speed of national change in attitude about homosexuality: "It's important for us to note the progress that's been made just in the last two and a half years."[37]

It's easy for us evangelicals to blame these changes on the president, individual politicians, the media, or even college professors. These changes actually appear to be the results of much larger forces and currents of national cultural change. The individuals whom we often credit with *causing* these changes are typically the second generation who were *taught* these changes earlier in their lives.

The culture is hurtling along at a rate of increasing change. Its direction clearly includes reactive anger against biblical Christians and aggressive promotion of the homosexual, bisexual, and transgender agenda. This rate of change will further accelerate with the passing of the two oldest generations in the United States.

3. The rate of the change toward this direction will further accelerate as the oldest two generations die.

For the next fifteen to twenty years, we will see continued conservative resistance to the tides of pro-homosexuality and anti-Christian prejudice. With each passing year, however, the resistance will seem weaker and weaker. It will seem more desperate and less relevant, because it will be.

The Americans who feel so strongly about these values are literally dying off and disappearing. In a big sense, their traditional American values will die with them. Even among Bible-believing evangelicals, the younger generations do not universally embrace these national cultural battles as their calling.

At some point in the next twenty years, probably sooner, the culture will turn a corner—at which point the same-sex marriage debates will be firmly decided among the supermajority of Americans.

At or soon after that time, this next point will be true.

4. These changes will reach a point at which they directly affect church as we know it and life for evangelical Christians as we know it.

When we examine the growth or shrinkage of the national church, we will see that perception is not reality. We will note the counterintuitive reality that, while the church nationally shrinks, most of us have moved to larger churches, which are attracting more believers from smaller churches. As a result, most of us have the *perception* that "the church" is growing, when in reality, she is not.

There is a similar disconnect of perception and reality with the changing hostile host culture. Most of us agree about the direction of the host culture. We see network television playing hypersexual and pro-homosexual shows that wouldn't have been imagined on HBO even a decade ago. Just months ago a new television show titled *Good Christian B_ _ _ _ es* was set to release. Due to last-minute boycotts, not only from Christians but also from women's groups who protested calling women the "B-word," executives changed the name to *Good Christian Belles* and then finally *GCB*. This isn't on MTV or VH1, but ABC—the same network that brought us *TGIF*, *Full House*, *Family Matters*, and a catalog of "family-friendly" programming just a couple of decades ago. Fittingly, the show was canceled after just ten episodes.

Not that children or teenagers are watching much ABC. They're feeding instead on a steady diet of hypersexual MTV, VH1, "uncut and unrated" films, and hardcore pornography—not only on Mom or Dad's flat-screen TVs, but also on the private 24/7 accessible screens of their phones and computers. I have nonreligious and agnostic friends who have worried aloud to me about the manic sexuality their children are growing up in.

The trend toward a hypersexual culture has been extensively documented and is so obvious that I won't bother to prove it here. Ed Stetzer gathered a few facts that demonstrate how widespread the trend is:

- Every thirty minutes a porn film is made in the United States.
- The United States produces 89 percent of all pornographic web pages.

- Every second, 30,000 people are viewing porn.
- 42.7 percent of Internet users view porn.
- The average age of initial pornography exposure is just eleven.[38]

As a result of those facts, it's not surprising that

- One-in-thirteen United States teen girls report participating in group sex, in a study that also links group sex to teens who excessively view pornography.[39]
- The average age of a first group-sex experience for a United States teen girl is 15.6 years old.[40]
- The City of Philadelphia has lowered the age for condom distribution to eleven years old, or fifth grade.[41]

If there's a Reformation or Renaissance being propelled by the new technologies of our age, it is not a Christian Reformation, but a re-forming of society into a culture of hedonistic and unrestrained sexuality and selfishness.

The 20th-century United States may not have been golden or perfect, but nobody would argue that it was as dark as what we're seeing today. Those in touch with younger Americans and their actual lives and media habits understand the hypersexuality of future America. If we think a culture can run this fast into the darkness and not radically change, we have not been reading our Bibles or our history books.

Most of us accept the direction and speed of these cultural changes—at least as abstract realities. Unfortunately, we sometimes see these changes as distant and harmless, perhaps because they are not yet affecting us personally. Our perception—the changes are abrupt but not all that bad—becomes our reality. Instead, we must step outside of our limited personal experience to see the actual reality, beyond our perception.

As we go about our routines, we are unlikely to see the unadvertised increases in human sex slavery in the United States, the rise in violent sex crimes, the rise in pedophilia as a generation attempts to replicate formative sexual encounters from preteen and teen years, or the other signs of a Sodom-and-Gomorrah-like culture that is saturating 21st-century America.

Few national observers connect these dots for us, but the link between excessive pornography use and pedophilia, rape, and violent sex crimes is well documented. As just one example, in 2012 a Los Angeles elementary school teacher was caught taking "bondage-type" photos of his seven- to ten-year-old students. When police searched his home, they found adult pornography depicting the exact same scenarios.[42]

Most of us evangelicals are at the far receiving end of these cultural changes. That is, we will be the last to be personally affected by mainstream cultural changes, and therefore the last to realize their magnitude.

Very few of us live in New York, Los Angeles, Washington DC, or Silicon Valley. Few of us work in public universities or at mainstream media outlets. However, the majority of influential culture shapers in our age do live and work in these areas. As such, we are out of touch with the mindset, worldview, and values of the relative few who frame the debates, shape the policies, and name the assumptions for America's developing generations.

I know these are simplistic, broad strokes. The point is that few of us will realize how quickly culture has changed until that change bleeds in from the coastal metropolises to the middle-American cities, comfortable suburbs, and insulated social circles we call home.

In other words, we won't realize that these irreversible cultural changes affect us—until they affect us. At that point it will be too late to be strategic as Christ's ambassadors.

We can't predict the future. We don't know if these cultural trends will ignore evangelicals, or if they will result in some churches being labeled "hate groups" and losing their tax-exempt status. We don't know if the APA will someday add "intolerant personality disorder" to its diagnostic manual, as some psychologists have suggested, or not.

What we do know is this. The trending trajectories and their speed of change indicate that in the coming decades, life for American evangelicals will be radically different than it is today. The host culture we find ourselves in is changing radically and rapidly. And we know that starting in 2013, it is a crime in California for a Christian counselor to help a teen not act on homosexual impulses, even if that teen wants such help.

The oak of evangelicalism in the United States is struggling with the rot of internal disease. A look at the horizon reveals she is also in for a big storm. Testing and tearing winds of tumultuous change will rip at her.

The natural, fear-based reaction to these changes is to raise our guard and fight for our rights. As we'll see in the next chapter, that reaction is dividing what remains of the evangelical church in the United States.

3

Dividing

If a house is divided against itself, that house cannot stand.

Mark 3:25

Gregory Boyd is not just a megachurch pastor who inherited a mammoth congregation. He is the man God used to grow Woodland Hills Church in Minnesota from forty people to five thousand.

With powerful worship and practical Bible teaching, Woodland Hills embodies the oft-idealized growing megachurch—with one slight tweak. A graduate of Yale Divinity School and Princeton Theological Seminary, Boyd isn't just a gifted communicator and pastor, he's also an Ivy League intellectual.

So when Boyd was pressured to introduce Republican politicians from the pulpit, he hesitated. The more his church grew, the more it seemed he was expected, perhaps required, to call his congregation to action for the evangelical right's agenda. Boyd felt trapped in a conflict between what he saw as Christ's kingdom and the kingdom of Republican politics.

On April 18, 2004, Boyd declared his loyalty. He preached a questioning sermon titled "Taking America Back for God?" He argued that the United States is not a Christian nation, saying, "The kingdom of God and the kingdom of this world are two very separate things. One uses the sword (power over) to influence people; the other uses love (power under)."[1]

Boyd was declaring his independence from the religious right. If there was any question about whose power and kingdom he belonged to, he clarified it: "I am sorry to tell you that America is not the light of the world and the hope of the world," he said. "The light of the world and the hope of the world is Jesus Christ."[2]

Boyd's sermon series and his subsequent book, *The Myth of a Christian Nation: How the Quest for Political Power Is Destroying the Church*, represent common sentiments in the growing evangelical split away from the political right.

About one thousand of Boyd's congregants left the church in protest after he claimed that America is not a Christian nation. That exodus is a small picture of the great divide splitting evangelicalism nationally. The *New York Times* accurately noted that Boyd and his church represent a divide in the national movement:

> The upheaval at Woodland Hills is an example of the internal debates now going on in some evangelical colleges, magazines and churches. A common concern is that the Christian message is being compromised by the tendency to tie evangelical Christianity to the Republican Party and American nationalism.[3]

As United States culture reacts to the religious right, many evangelicals are splitting away from the right—not always because they disagree with its positions, but often because they disagree with its methods, priorities, or message to Americans at large. Even as the majority of young, coastal, and metropolitan evangelicals split from the evangelical right, the right itself remains an established, large, wealthy, and powerful chunk of evangelicalism.

This gaping political divide is just one of the fissures splitting evangelicalism. The more we attempt to respond to a rapidly changing culture, the more we seem to be fighting and dividing ourselves over how to be Christ's presence in a brave new world.

The Split Will Amplify in Coming Decades, Thus Weakening an Already Crippled Church

We're barely into the 21st century, and it's apparent that the unified evangelicalism of the 20th century is a thing of the past. Evangelicals are dividing and not conquering over a number of issues: politics, theology, church models and methods, views of Scripture, new approaches to the atonement. The list goes on.

Of course, evangelicals have always been a diverse and opinionated bunch. What was unique about 20th-century evangelicalism was its broad mainstream unity around the gospel, best represented in the person and ministry of Billy Graham.

New York Times reporter Michael Luo rightly identifies that as Graham's influence fades, so does the movement's unity. The precise evangelical focus on the gospel has been lost in the muddy waters of politics, culture wars, and progressive theology.

Luo asked Roger E. Olson, a professor at Baylor University's Truett Theological Seminary, about post-Graham evangelicalism. Olson said, "When he leaves the scene, there will be some deep fractures that come out into the open and become wider. It will be harder for anyone to talk about evangelicalism as a movement with any unity."[4]

Entire books are being written about these fractures. In this chapter, we'll demonstrate the trend of internal divisions by examining just one fracture—political splinters within the church.

The point here is not that all evangelicals should see eye-to-eye on politics or other issues. The point is that our great strength in the 20th century was our unity, our ability to agree to disagree and then work together in Christ's name for the gospel. We are losing that cohesion. And with it, we are losing our greatest strength at the time of our greatest strain and struggle.

In the face of declining numbers (Sputtering), failing discipleship (Bleeding), depleted dollars (Bankrupt), and an antagonistic host culture (Hated), the once-unified movement of 20th-Century Evangelicalism is dividing itself into a less powerful, less unified, and less organized movement. At the moment when we most need the strength of our unity, we are voluntarily abandoning it.

Theologically, internal disputes are erupting, even as the outer boundaries of doctrine are dissolving. We'll further address the trend of theological disputes in one of the later "solution" chapters (Uniting). In this chapter, though, let's examine the political divisions within evangelicalism—as one example of the fissures in the foundation of United States evangelicalism.

Who Is Splitting Away From the Political Right?

Politically, more United States evangelicals are trying to rebrand the movement, or at least themselves—to draw attention *away from* politics and *toward* Jesus. (Note: within this chapter, when I use the terms *right*, *left*, and *middle*, I mean politically right, left, or middle, not theologically.)

Those splitting away from the religious right fall into two groups. A growing evangelical left is reacting to the right's assumed monopoly over evangelicalism. Simultaneously, an informal but gigantic group of less political evangelicals is also splitting away from the right. I call this group the moderate middle. They are not necessarily left, but would prefer to focus all the political energy on spreading the gospel. This informal group is poised to become the mainstream of 21st-Century Evangelicalism.

Even as these two groups splinter away, the right itself is, in the assessment of many, moving further to the right—likely as a reaction to the startling changes taking place in the culture. The political right wing of evangelicalism is struggling and literally dying off, but it still holds much of the money, institutional influence, and resolve. It will remain wealthy and powerful as it struggles through the next two decades.

Those splitting from the religious right are generally more directly involved with secular Americans and their perceptions. In their book *unChristian*, researchers David Kinnaman and Gabe Lyons concluded, "Christians are now perceived among Mosaics and Busters as too involved in politics. To be more precise, they think of us as motivated primarily by political goals and as promoting a right-wing agenda."[5]

Many evangelicals are pushing back against these political associations. More young evangelical leaders see it as crucial to separate politics from Jesus—so that lost souls don't reject Jesus simply because they think He is a Republican.

For the most part, the evangelical split from the right toes generational lines (younger evangelicals are moving away from the right), geographic lines (coastal and metropolitan evangelicals are less likely to identify with the right), and educational lines (highly educated evangelicals are also less likely to identify with the right).

Left evangelicals, like Pastor Greg Boyd, are boldly speaking out. The greater migration, however, is less boisterous and less noticed. Entire chunks of the evangelical church are silently and informally disassociating from the political agenda of the right, drifting into the moderate middle.

As early as 2004, Pew researcher and professor John C. Green spotted the decline of the evangelical right. He found statistically that when combined, politically left and moderate middle evangelicals slightly outnumbered right evangelicals. Here's the percentage of evangelicals loyal to the left, right, and middle, as of 2004:[6]

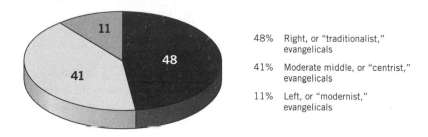

48% Right, or "traditionalist," evangelicals

41% Moderate middle, or "centrist," evangelicals

11% Left, or "modernist," evangelicals

When combined, moderate middle and left evangelicals accounted for 52 percent of the movement, in 2004.

In 2005, nearly as many evangelicals identified themselves as either Democrat or Independent (47 percent total) as Republican (54 percent), according to a Gallup poll.[7] By 2007, sociologist Michael Lindsay reported, "Fully 70 percent of evangelicals in America do not identify with the religious right."[8]

If generational trends are any indication, this reaction to right-wing politics will entrench itself as the dominant strain of evangelicalism in the next twenty years, but the transition of the movement is proving to be bloody and difficult.

Unfortunately, as various evangelicals splinter away from and react to each other politically, the tone is one of hurt, betrayal, and disappointment. Evangelicals who disagree on politics often fall into combative roles, rather than complementary ones. With good intentions, many evangelicals have elevated political positions to the level of spiritual and theological orthodoxy. Leaders and ministries that mean well are infighting—dividing what remains of a vulnerable church in the first years of the 21st century.

It's not uncommon to open a mainstream newspaper and find right or left evangelicals criticizing their "opponents" in the national news. Take for example, a *New York Times* article where the representative of a large evangelical organization blasts Jim Wallis about abortion, claiming he doesn't care about "45 million babies killed." That punch from the right, toward the left, is mirrored by a separate op-ed from two middle or left evangelical professors who name and critique three "stubborn anti-intellectuals" from the evangelical right, not in an evangelical journal but also in the *New York Times*.[9] These jabs come from both sides and represent the pronounced divides in a once-unified movement.

Individual local pastors like Greg Boyd are leading their congregations away from the right. So are national mainstream leaders. In the last decade, no rising evangelical star has been an activist for the right. Some old leaders from the 1980s and 1990s are still reaffirming their agenda, and politicians like Sarah Palin and Rick Perry wear the evangelical badge. But we are hard pressed to think of a recent mainstream spiritual leader of influence who is picking up where Falwell, Dobson, and Robertson left off.

Cal Thomas is a different kind of national evangelical leader—one who was at the helm of the evangelical right and now sees it as a harmful and distracting cause. As a Washington DC insider, Fox News personality, syndicated newspaper columnist, and former

Moral Majority vice president, Thomas has seen firsthand the best and worst of politics for decades.

Thomas emphasizes Jesus' claim that His "kingdom is not of this world" (John 18:36). That's a common priority in the moderate middle position, and it's eloquently explained in the book he wrote with Ed Dobson, *Blinded by Might: Why the Religious Right Can't Save America*.

Thomas's moderate middle position is well described in this *Newsweek* column:

> The columnist Cal Thomas was an early figure in the Moral Majority who came to see the Christian American movement as fatally flawed in theological terms. "No country can be truly 'Christian,'" Thomas says. "Only people can. God is above all nations, and, in fact, Isaiah says that 'All nations are to him a drop in the bucket and less than nothing.'" Thinking back across the decades, Thomas recalls the hope—and the failure. "We were going through organizing like-minded people to 'return' America to a time of greater morality. Of course, this was to be done through politicians who had a difficult time imposing morality on themselves!"[10]

The sexual affairs of religious right politicians like Senator John Ensign, Governor Mark Sanford, and Congressman Chip Pickering demonstrate Thomas's point. For the evangelical right to lecture the world on morality seems increasingly hypocritical. The gay prostitute scandal of homosexual marriage opponent and evangelical figurehead Ted Haggard may have marked the low point for the right, as it fights accusations of hypocrisy.

Thomas is not alone in his move from the right to the moderate middle. When pastor Rick Warren hosted Democratic candidate Barack Obama at Saddleback Church (for which he has received plenty of criticism), Warren was signaling that his brand of evangelicalism is not owned by the GOP. The same was true when Warren partnered with Obama to fight AIDS in Africa, a move derided by right evangelicals. The evangelical right also criticized Warren for his involvement in "The ONE Campaign: To Make Poverty History."

Andy Stanley has invited Michelle Obama to speak from his pulpit. Bill Hybels and National Association of Evangelicals president Leith Anderson have also modeled a growing moderate middle position. They attended one of Obama's speeches about immigration overhaul, expressing their personal support for immigrants. That's exactly the opposite view of the position strongly held by the established right and conservative Republicans.[11]

The pastors, writers, and professors leading the retreat from the right are generally coastal or metropolitan. Evangelicals from other countries, like Alister McGrath, also struggle to understand why American evangelicalism has been so tied to Republican politics.

Many moderates see politics as a lower priority *because of* their rich theology, not for lack of it. For example, nobody would argue that pastor-teacher John MacArthur is theologically liberal. In his book *Why Government Can't Save You: An Alternative to Political Activism*, MacArthur argues for the moderate middle position, as summarized in the two quotes below:

> Rather than demanding our rights and creating for ourselves a world where we feel safe and accepted, we need to see the deep spiritual needs of the world and concern ourselves with offering people hope through Jesus Christ. That's what being a living sacrifice is all about.[12]

> It is all right occasionally to support legitimate measures designed to correct a glaring social or political wrong . . . as long as we realize that such interest is not vital to our spiritual lives, our righteous testimony or the advancement of the kingdom of Christ. Above all, the believer's political involvement should never displace the priority of preaching and teaching the gospel because the morality and righteousness that God seeks is the result of salvation and sanctification.[13]

The Mainstream Evangelical Agenda Has Shifted From Politics to Social Justice

In addition to the lead of politically moderate middle personalities like Rick Warren, Bill Hybels, and John MacArthur, a wave of scriptural social justice is also sweeping United States evangelicalism. The social justice trend is out of step with the right for a few reasons. Most notably, it is changing evangelical focus, not only away from United States politics, but away from the United States altogether.

Compared to the evangelical focus ten years ago, the conversation today is less about "defending" America and more about providing for those who are starving and dying apart from Christ on other continents.

The new leaders of evangelicalism are driving this surge in scriptural social justice, as evidenced in bestsellers like David Platt's *Radical*, Tim Keller's *Generous Justice*, and Max Lucado's *Outlive Your Life*. These books demonstrate the mainstream movement's adoption of an agenda that simply ignores the evangelical right agenda of the 1980s to early 2000s.

This burgeoning biblical social justice movement is tapping in to a throbbing artery near the heart of younger evangelicals.

Younger Evangelicals Are Also Stepping Away From the Political Right

In addition to pastors and national leaders, younger evangelicals are also abandoning the evangelical right. PBS reports:

> Not only are they [young evangelicals] more liberal on several of the hot button issues currently driving conservative politics, many evangelicals in Generation Next want to change the conversation altogether, putting traditionally left-leaning concerns such as the environment and social justice to the forefront of the evangelical movement.[14]

A 2007 Pew Research Center report documented younger evangelicals and their move away from the GOP:

> White evangelicals are typically analyzed as a group, but an examination of the younger generation (those ages 18–29) provides evidence that white evangelicals may be undergoing some significant

political changes. . . . Younger white evangelicals have become increasingly dissatisfied . . . and are moving away from the GOP.[15]

Here's what the Pew Research Center found. In 2001, 55 percent of young evangelicals were Republicans. By 2005, that had dropped to only 40 percent being Republican. In the same time, older evangelicals also decreased their loyalty to the Republican Party, though by only 5 percent, versus the younger generation's 15 percent decrease.[16]

The current of evangelicals rushing toward the middle and left has flowed into publishing, too. A flood of post-right-wing books has swamped the evangelical market, and its waters continue to rise. Most often, devout younger evangelicals are writing about the emotional strain that their differing political views brings to their relationships with family and church.

Alisa Harris's book, *Raised Right: How I Untangled My Faith from Politics*, is one example of this new genre. Some of the most spiritually devoted young evangelicals are the most dedicated to parsing out politics from Christ's message.

"*Raised Right* demonstrates that the evangelical stampede to the far right in the 1980s has produced a generational backlash, as young evangelicals like Alisa Harris encounter the Hebrew prophets and the words of Jesus. This is the most encouraging book about evangelicals and politics I have read in a very long time,"[17] writes Randall Balmer, a leading evangelical scholar and author of *Thy Kingdom Come: How the Religious Right Distorts the Faith and Threatens America*.

Jim Wallis, often referred to as a leader of the evangelical left, has long taken an active role in politics. Here's his recent observation about younger evangelicals, as he interacts with them across the United States:

> The young people I meet don't want to go Left or Right. They reject these narrow political orthodoxies. . . . Instead, young evangelicals . . . want their love of Jesus to express itself in the world, in relationship to other people, and in the pressing demands and problems of the world. I find this to be true among younger and younger people.[18]

Academic Evangelicals Are Stepping Away From the Political Right

The trend among many evangelical academic leaders is also away from the right. One notable exception is Dr. Wayne Grudem, who eloquently defends and explains dozens of politically right evangelical positions in *Politics—According to the Bible*. As with all of Grudem's work, the book is handsomely thorough, precise, and rigorous.

Mark Noll, Nathan Hatch, and George Marsden represent a moderate middle position in their book, *The Search for Christian America*. They write, "[Christians] should not have illusions about the nature of human governments. Ultimately they belong to what Augustine calls 'the city of the world,' in which self-interest rules . . . all governments can be brutal killers."[19]

They add:

> We have important obligations to do whatever we can, including through the use of political means, to help our neighbors—promoting just laws, good order, peace, education and opportunity. Nonetheless we should recognize that as we work for the relatively better in "the city of the world," our successes will be just that—relative. In the last analysis the church declares that the solutions offered by the nations of the world are always transitory solutions, themselves in need of reform.[20]

Their sentiments represent the moderate middle position. Many moderates still vote toward right-wing values. They see democracy as something to steward through voting, but that's often the extent of their political involvement. And they believe that were Jesus physically in the United States today, it would be the extent of His political involvement, too.

The Fastest Growing Group of Evangelicals—Non-Whites—Is Also Resisting the Political Right

The fastest growing segment in the evangelical church is also less likely to agree with the evangelical right. As our national movement bleeds out its own children (see chapter 5, Bleeding), congregations that embrace immigrants are seeing consistent new-believer growth from the Hispanic population, a group that adds about one million new United States residents every year.

Richard Land is a national leader with the Southern Baptist Convention. He points out the irony that the evangelical right is resisting immigrants, even as Hispanics prove to be the bright spot in church growth. Land is one of many national leaders who are stepping away from the right in order to reach out to the immigrant community.

"I've had some older conservative leaders say: 'Richard, stop this. You're going to split the conservative coalition,'" Dr. Land said in a July 18, 2010, *New York Times* article. He added, "You don't get a lot of Hispanics in your coalition by engaging in anti-Hispanic anti-immigration rhetoric."[21]

Southern Baptists aren't the only evangelical group aware of Hispanic growth. As of 2011, "America's largest Assemblies of God congregation is Hispanic—the 11,000-member New Life Covenant Church in Chicago," according to Beliefnet.[22]

Moderate and left evangelicals point to New Testament Scripture as a call to embrace immigrants spiritually, regardless of their immigration status. They argue that evangelical Christian growth has always thrived on society's fringes and outcasts. For example, in Colossians 3:11, Paul reminds the New Testament church "there is no Greek or Jew, circumcised or uncircumcised, barbarian, Scythian, slave or free, but Christ is all, and is in all."

Evangelical scholar Soong-Chan Rah put it this way: "Contrary to popular opinion, the Church is not dying in America; it is alive and well, but it is alive and well among the immigrant and ethnic minority communities and not among the majority white churches in the United States."[23]

The Religious Right, Fading but Still an Inextricable Part of United States Evangelical DNA

The right may be losing its assumed hold on evangelicalism, but it still accounts for about half of the movement. Moreover, it holds a disproportionately large share of influence, position, and wealth, particularly in middle and southern states. The settled power base of the right chides against the new ideas of the evangelical left and moderate middle. As a result, this trend of political divisions is likely to continue splitting churches, ministries, and families for the next twenty years. Evangelicals across the country will continue disagreeing on contradictory answers to the same question: "How do we respond to this rapidly changing culture?"

In 2007, the once-powerful Center for Reclaiming America closed its doors. The shuttering of Dr. D. James Kennedy's political organization was indicative of the struggle the right faces as its founders (and key fundraisers) age and pass away. As *Newsweek* put it, "By 2006 the religious right was in disarray. Falwell would die the following year, and Dobson and Robertson were widely regarded as dinosaurs."[24]

Even as the fathers of the evangelical right pass on or fade into irrelevance, their call to political activism remains an inextricable thread in our movement's DNA. Evangelicals who witnessed the political victories of the 1980s still believe that God is waiting to work through our political activism, if we will join Him.

Many in the right wholeheartedly believe that evangelicals elected Reagan, that we elected Bush, and that, if younger evangelicals would get on board, we could turn the nation around by means of political involvement. How disheartening and terrifying it is for these faithful evangelicals to see the younger church abandoning the causes to which they gave their lives and much of their wealth. The right, while weakened, remains an influential and faithful force of great power within evangelicalism.

The Trajectory of Increasing Divisions Within United States Evangelicalism

This chapter touches on a nationwide debate that deserves entire books of treatment. The point here is not to opine which political group is "correct"—left, moderate middle, or right. The point here is a simple observation: The United States Church is crippled, declining, bleeding, broke, and despised, and the remaining church is dividing herself over United States politics. This is just one of the chasms splitting the movement.

We have seen that our movement is smaller than we thought and that the leading edges of the host culture are turning antagonistic toward us. We will also see that we're losing most of our kids, and that our evangelism efforts are not keeping pace with population growth. Next, we will see that the fuel our national machine runs on—dollars—is drying up and disappearing. In the midst of all this, or actually as a result of all this, the unified evangelicalism of the 20th century is splintering and fraying, turning against itself.

Political divisions are nothing new in United States churches. What is new is that as the church divides herself over politics, she does not enjoy the cultural clout, the robust health, or the hospitable host culture that she had during the political divisions of past centuries.

For two reasons, these growing divisions will further split the evangelical church during the next decades.

1. The increasing speed of cultural change will amplify these splits, displacing these groups further and further apart.

Evangelical scholar D. A. Carson has correctly observed:

> Doubtless there have always been generational conflicts of one sort or another. Arguably, however, in some ways they are becoming worse. . . . The rate of cultural change has sped up, making it far more difficult for older people to empathize with a world so very different from the one in which they grew up three or four decades earlier.[25]

The divisions we're seeing today result from radically conflicting answers to the same question: "How do we respond to the changing culture?" That question will become increasingly difficult to answer as the culture continues its accelerating change.

In simple, broad strokes, here's what we are already seeing and can likely expect to continue seeing: Younger, coastal, highly educated, and metropolitan evangelicals feel more and more strongly that we should abandon political rhetoric and elevate the gospel by focusing on Jesus' message to a post-Christian culture that is not home. They see the marriage of Jesus and the American flag as a pollution of Christ, as nationalistic static and extra noise that distracts from Jesus and His kingdom.

At the same time, frightened by changes in United States culture, middle-American, Bible-belt, suburban, and older evangelicals feel more and more strongly that we need to "defend" our rights in "our Christian nation." They believe that we and our elected officials are called to hold back the tide of spiritual darkness through political influence. They see the increasingly hostile host culture as a reason for further political activism, not less.

These groups will split further and further apart as the culture continues changing. Their reactionary distancing will continue, because they have differing foundational views about two emotionally charged issues. First, they strongly disagree about America's present status as a Christian nation. They also have conflicting foundational views about Christ's methods and means for redeeming a culture—whether human government is central to God's plan today or peripheral to it.

2. Evangelicalism will continue fraying and splintering for another reason: postmodern influence on individual thought.

When previous generations of evangelicals had differences, they shared a common grid through which to interpret the changes and challenges of their day.

As a result of that shared grid, evangelical splits have resulted in cleanly categorized groups: Calvinist and Arminian; covenant and dispensational; pre-, post-, and a-millennial; Southern and Northern Baptists, fundamentalists and neo-evangelicals; and so forth.

The splits in the 21st-century church will not be so clean, because younger evangelicals defy categorization and resist labels. For example, young evangelicals are fleeing the Republican Party in droves, but they aren't abandoning it to become Democrats. They're registering as independents. Where one "independent" evangelical believes the government should provide social services for the poor, another "independent" believes such services are Marxist and not the government's role. But both refuse to define themselves as Democrat or Republican.

Given the individualistic, postmodern DNA embedded in younger evangelicals, I expect evangelicalism may split into dozens or hundreds of new small- and medium-sized, overlapping, and sometimes chaotic groups. The result could be a completely disorganized and un-unified national church.

Such splits may prove to be just as common in theology as in politics. Rob Bell's questioning of the atonement in *Love Wins*, and the evangelical community's response to it, demonstrate there is no longer a single "modern" grid or orthodox worldview lens through which evangelicals see the United States, the church, or the Bible.

Even as we wrestle with daunting new questions, the ground beneath our feet is moving. The theological and cultural mores that were "givens" for evangelicals just fifteen years ago are no longer givens. Everything is up for debate. Nothing can be taken for granted. Truth is up for grabs.

Indeed, this reality, in combination with the other trends noted in this book, should sober and humble us as we prayerfully lead Christ's bride further into the 21st century.

As leaders who are Bell's age and younger increasingly take the reins, we may see postmodern subjectivity and pluralism blended more and more with evangelical theology, practice, and politics. This will be done more informally than formally. Old heresies will resurface as exciting new ideas. Inerrancy will be doubted and written off by some younger evangelicals who will mean well as they lead churches into that deadly error.

D. A. Carson spotted this when he stated, "There are many people today who call themselves evangelical whom no person would call an evangelical 40 years ago."[26]

Theologically conservative evangelicals will either take a bunker mentality and allow the movement to drift into pluralism, or they will push against these changes and purify the movement, hopefully in a spirit of grace and love. In either case, the already splintered movement will likely continue fraying to further extremes—dividing itself over politics, theology, and practice.

Nobody can foretell precisely how the evangelical church will splinter or what the end results will be. What we can safely observe is that the somewhat unified movement of the 20th century is on a trajectory of division, disunification, and rupture.

The United States evangelical church has ruptured before, but never in the face of such internal decline and such external opposition.

4

Bankrupt

The prudent see danger and take refuge, but the simple keep
going and suffer for it.

Proverbs 27:12

On December 5, 2010, Phoenix pastor Mark Martin told a story.
He stood on the stage at Calvary Community, a church that claims
12,000 attendees, and explained the plight of a close friend.

"There's someone that most of you know that really has a need.
She's been going through a huge trial the past couple of years,
but she hasn't wanted to say anything to anybody about it. . . .
She wouldn't tell you what's going on, but I know you'd want to
know," Martin explained.[1]

Families wondered if they knew the woman. Had they worshiped
next to her? Bumped into her in the nursery?

"This last year she lost a third of her income. And what grieves
me is that she's been so generous to others . . . a whole lot of people
depend on her," he continued.

"I know it's Christmastime, and a lot of us are looking for ways
that we might be able to, you know, spread the love of Jesus. But
frankly, I know that the reality is she's gonna need some long-term

support. And for those of you who would like to help"— Martin paused—"her name is Calvary."

The friend was Calvary Community Church, *their* church. Her income was decreasing year after year, the pastor said. In two previous years the megachurch had seen a 25 percent decrease each year. But the last year was even worse. Giving decreased by another 30 percent.

Martin was speaking of his own specific congregation, but he might as well have been talking about the national United States church. He was talking about the fiscal year of 2010, but he might as well have been talking about the years of 2013, 2014, and on through the next decade.

Creative calls for increased giving, like Martin's, will become familiar in the next few years—even from thriving churches, like Martin's, and other ministries that have not historically issued such pleas. Donations to many churches and ministries have plummeted 20 to 30 percent each year since the Great Recession pummeled the United States economy.

We often tie the drop in giving to the drop in the economy. But a larger undercurrent is also at play. The generation that gives almost half of total donations began passing away about three years ago. Nearly one thousand of them are called home every day. Their funerals and memorials are quietly held every morning, afternoon, and evening in rural churches and metropolitan chapels across the country. Nobody seems to be noticing.

Over the next twelve years, this faithful and reliable generation will pass away. As they do, total giving will decrease by as much as half for typical evangelical ministries—nationally, regionally, and locally.[2]

Budgets will fall short. Pastors and national leaders will employ 20th-century tactics that used to work in times of financial emergency.

- They will preach direct messages about stewardship.
- They will direct letters and emails to donors.
- They will make sure that reliable givers get a personal phone call.

These methods will not work for the same reason that the Block-buster store near you—the one that buzzed with movie renters just five years ago—is now vacant. The methods will not work because they are 20th-century methods in a 21st-century world. Responsible leaders must embrace this reality now and begin planning accordingly.

Within decades we will see the closures or radical downsizings of some juggernaut ministries. We're already seeing some of those closures. In early 2011, the fleet of yellow golf carts that once buzzed around the forty-acre campus at Robert Schuller's Crystal Cathedral sat empty and idle.

The thirteen-story Tower of Hope still stood as majestic as it did in 1968, when Schuller dedicated the property to God's glory. But the tower and the thousands of glass panes in the cathedral had never been so dirty.

In 2010 the Crystal Cathedral stopped paying its dozens of maintenance workers. The cost of maintenance was minimal compared to the $48 million debt the ministry had accrued as giving dived around 2009. By 2011, the ministry could not pay its janitors. It filed for Chapter 11 bankruptcy.

"The church saw revenue drop roughly 30 percent in 2009 and simply couldn't slash expenses quickly enough to avoid accruing the debt," according to Pastor Jim Penner.[3]

Schuller has swelled into tears on more than one occasion, delivering heartfelt appeals for money from the pulpit. "I need more help from you. If you are a tither, become a double-tither. If you are not a tither, become a tither," he has begged.[4] The evangelical icon's pleas for help have failed to pull the church out of bankruptcy.

Schuller's Crystal Cathedral, while certainly unique, has for decades been a forerunner and trendsetter for the nation's other megachurches. Now, according to statistics, its bankruptcy demonstrates where thousands of other churches may be in twenty years, or sooner.

From young, thriving, and conservative ministries to established evangelical mainstays of all stripes, the financial strain of the Great Evangelical Recession is beginning to show in desperate funding pleas from all manner of ministries.

The traceable trend is that giving is dropping severely across the United States. Already a handful of national ministries are collapsing under donation shortages. Pat Robertson's Regent University recently required a "$95 million booster shot from the Christian Broadcasting Network" to continue operating.[5] Another force that once seemed invincible, D. James Kennedy's Center for Reclaiming America, closed its Washington DC office in 2007.[6]

Such collapses will be commonplace in 21st-Century Evangelicalism—unless generational giving patterns change radically. Ministries like Schuller's, Robertson's, and Kennedy's are but the first wave of a donation recession that will afflict most ministries, regardless of size, and topple the global evangelical culture as we know it.

Simply put, the older contributors who fund evangelical ministries are passing off the scene. It is a fact that, on the whole, their kids and grandkids do not share their commitment to evangelical ministries (if their heirs are evangelical at all, as we will see in chapter 5, Bleeding).

Unless giving trends change significantly, evangelical giving across the board may drop by about 70 percent during the next twenty-five to thirty years. A recovery of the United States economy will not have bearing on dropping ministry income—unless generational patterns change drastically.

This continuing decrease will challenge the most creative and forward-thinking ministries, and it will bankrupt the unprepared. A great crisis of funding is swelling on the horizon—a silent tsunami that has already broken—unnoticed and miles off the coast. Most ministries are entirely unprepared.

We have seen that United States evangelicalism—while still a massive movement—is a fraction of the size that many of us believed it to be. In upcoming chapters we'll see that the movement is also shrinking, slowly. Now let's diagnose the practical engine of the American evangelical machine. Those enmeshed in the cogs and machinery of evangelical ministries know that practically the entire machine runs on one common fuel: dollars.

The unannounced reality is that evangelical dollars have been steadily declining for years in the United States. The economic recession accelerated that decline, but recession giving is a boon compared to the forecast for the upcoming decades.

Four factors are leading to a severe fuel crisis in the church. Barring radical, unforeseen changes, the combined trends below will collapse or seriously cripple the machine of American evangelicalism, as we know it. Here's why:

1. Our ministry model has become overly dependent on dollars.
2. Giving on the whole has been decreasing for years.
3. Donations are on course to drop by about 70 percent within twenty-five to thirty years—due to the deaths of the most generous generations.
4. Each ensuing generation in the church is increasingly unreliable, unpredictable, and less generous in their giving, when compared to the previous generation.

1. Dependence on dollars in the American evangelical church

While many church and ministry leaders cannot tell you the number of disciples they have made or nurtured in a year, almost all of them can tell you the number of dollars they need or have in hand.

This is not necessarily because they are greedy or have wrong motives. It is because they are American and have been trained to do ministry in an American, dollar-centric paradigm.

Our failure to generate and/or retain disciples in the American evangelical church (as will be demonstrated in chapter 5, Bleeding) has *not* been for lack of funding. American evangelicals give more than $12 billion to churches, parachurches, and mission agencies every year, by modest estimation.[7]

Somewhere along the way, unofficially and probably with good intentions, our ministry leaders began counting dollars instead of disciples. It is an Americanization, a dollar-centric deformity of the gospel. Whether intentional or not, dollar dependence in our host culture has led to an assumed dependence on the dollar to fulfill a commission that originally had nothing to do with material wealth.

Unawares, most of us have bought in to a profoundly American measure of what makes Christ's body and his agents "healthy" or "successful." We may not preach it from pulpits, but we assume it in board meetings. If we are in the black financially, then we must be doing okay.

In the book *More Money, More Ministry: Money and Evangelicals in Recent North American History*, Joel Carpenter writes a chapter about American evangelical church leaders who have been convinced that success depends on dollars.

> The vast majority of ministry leaders would never subscribe to a prosperity gospel ideology, but they are deeply infused with an American capitalist cultural understanding of the gospel—that God measures success by the numbers, that more money means more ministry, which means more success for God's kingdom.
>
> So they tend to measure their own success as disciples and servants of the Lord by the size of their ministry. The ones whose ministries command millions are introduced on the prayer breakfast rostrums as God's "choice servants." . . . American Christians are material creatures.[8]

Like most church trends, we discover how we got here by digging deeper into church history, particularly into the missionary-sending movements of the 19th and early 20th centuries.[9]

The unintended result of this fervent season in American missions was—and to this day is—a sort of class divide in the American church, between "goers" and "senders."[10] That is to say, the professional, or "goer," Christians are charged with doing the "real" work of evangelism and discipleship. This supported class includes missionaries, pastors, evangelists, professors, parachurch employees, and so forth—all the professional Christians.

The other class of American evangelicals is charged with financially supporting the goers—and in so doing, they have their hand in the fruit of new believers and disciples.

This Christian class divide created an entire ministry paradigm, which to this day underlies American evangelicalism. Many forward-thinking Christian leaders still assume this paradigm—paid Christian leaders and unpaid "laypeople."

Many of the most committed, gifted, and passionate evangelicals in the United States are in full-time, vocational work—or they are training for it. Most are untrained to make a living in

America without support from donors. Meanwhile, the other class of evangelicals has not been relied on for serious evangelism or discipleship. They are not expected to, or in many cases trained to, do these basic works.

So long as the "sending" or giving class continues providing enough dollars to support the goers, then American evangelicalism can continue at its current rate of gradual decline (documented in chapter 6, Sputtering).

However, if the donation dollars continue drying up, dropping off, and disappearing, the evangelical machine *as we know it* will bind and seize. We saw a preview of this when the financial recession hit church budgets. Barna found, "With churches cutting back on staff during 2007 through 2010, thousands of seminary-trained pastors were let go, with few openings available."[11]

The layoffs of the recession may be a foreshadowing of the evangelical layoffs coming in the next decades, as budgets decrease unexpectedly and radically. More pastors, teachers, and professors will have to leave traditional ministry to make ends meet.

A galaxy of parachurches, radio stations, and missions agencies—particularly the smaller and midsize ones—will simply dissolve as donations continue disappearing. Armed with bequeathals and trusts, the larger organizations will survive, but only by cutting budgets 50 to 70 percent, resulting in widespread "professional" Christian layoffs. The full force of this church recession may hit within the next decades.

The movement will be left in a precarious position. The "professional" Christians who are best trained to do the works of evangelism and discipleship will be scrambling to make a living. At the same time, the "sending" class of American evangelicals remains largely untrained in serious evangelism and discipleship.

2. The trend of overall decreased giving

Christ's original commission was not about dollars, and yet, the practical reality is that the majority of legitimate discipleship-making ministries in United States evangelicalism run, humanly speaking, on the fuel of donation dollars.

And so, the prospect of the church losing half of her donations is a fearful prospect, to say the least. Indeed, the landscape of American evangelicalism could be altered beyond recognition by this one factor.

A global network of ministries—from the Navigators and Campus Crusade for Christ to missions agencies, social justice works, radio stations, colleges, seminaries, national teaching ministries, and local churches—is effectively translating dollars into disciples. The majority of them could not bear the fruit they bear without millions of dollars in donations. And the majority of them, while successful now, do not have a paradigm for successful ministry without millions of donor dollars. Presently, the only go-to solution for ministries with declining donations is to somehow increase donations or to cut staff and facilities.

It is impossible to calculate the net global spiritual impact of American evangelical dollars. What can be calculated is that loads of money haven't kept evangelicalism in the United States from shrinking at home. Despite the billions invested over the past fifty years, evangelicalism has not kept pace with population growth in the United States (discussed in chapter 6, Sputtering).

Why is it that when evangelicals in the United States have more wealth, assets, and technology than the evangelical church has ever had in history, the church is declining at home? Somehow our employment of this wealth has not been fruitful enough to hold our ground at home.

Consider this: If we take the most modest estimate of the combined annual giving by American evangelicals, they give more than the gross domestic product of Iceland.[12] If nationalized, the combined annual giving of American evangelicals right now would likely be among the hundred largest economies in the world. And yet, we are not even holding our ground in the United States.

While our hope should not be placed in these dollars, the thought of American evangelical ministries attempting to function without funds is devastating. Such a drought of dollars would certainly accelerate the decline of evangelicalism as we know it. If we actually lose half of all gifts in the next thirty years, the consequences will be catastrophic. Half of the pastors you know would be unemployed, as well as half of the professors, parachurch employees, and so forth.

And that is the likely future. Multiple studies from the last decades and from recent years (even pre-recession) indicate that giving is consistently decreasing. This is not a coincidence. The amount of giving parallels, by generation, the commitment and spiritual maturity of the "sending" evangelicals. The newest generations, weaned by a consumer culture both inside and outside the church, have little concept of consistent or sacrificial giving.

The first decade of this new century demonstrates the disturbing dip in giving. Some decline obviously results from the economic recession, but a number of studies show that giving was decreasing year-over-year during the "boom" years that preceded the recession. As American evangelicals were refinancing their homes, sometimes pulling out tens of thousands of dollars in cash, their giving continued to decrease.

I am not aware of any reason to believe that this broad downward trend of giving, which was well under way before the recession, will reverse when or if the United States economy recovers.

Consider these giving findings, which preceded the recession:

2001: "Income Up, Giving Down: In 2001 members of evangelical churches gave away on average 4.27 percent of their income, down from 4.74 percent in 1985 and 6.15 percent in 1968, though annual household income has been steadily rising since 1968, even when adjusted for inflation."[13] That rate has since fallen to about 3 percent, which the younger generations consider "sacrificial."[14]

2003: Tithing decreased 62 percent from the previous year.[15]

2004: "In 2004 the church reached its lowest level of giving as a percentage of income since 1961, or lower than the worst years of the Great Depression. While evangelical Protestants continue to give more as a percentage of income than their mainline Protestant counterparts, evangelicals registered a steeper decline in giving. . . ."[16]

2005: The amount of giving, as a sum and as a percentage, decreased yet again.[17] Brian Kluth, president of the Christian Stewardship Association, observed a number of giving trends in the American evangelical church. He noted a decrease in (1) the percentage of income that Christians give, (2) the percentage of Christians giving at least 10 percent of their incomes, and (3) a clear understanding of the word "stewardship."[18]

Of course, some ministries will always be surging financially—attracting a larger share of the pie, even as the pie itself shrinks. Those presently in surging ministries should know your experience is not the national trend.

3. The death of the biggest giving generation

Despite decreases in the last decade, the American evangelical church remains a financial juggernaut. North American evangelicals, while accounting for less than 20 percent of the global evangelical church, hold 80 percent of global evangelical wealth.[19] In all, one simply cannot estimate the global spiritual ramifications if the network of American evangelicals were to collapse or be crippled for lack of funding.

But this is our most likely future. By multiple accounts, American evangelical donations are on course to drop by almost half in the next fourteen years and by two-thirds in the next thirty years.

The numbers on generational giving are stark. Folks over age 75 give four times as much of their income as 25- to 44-year-olds, according to *The State of Church Giving Through 2009*. Each younger generation gives significantly less of its income to ministry.

Percentage of Income Contributed to Church and Religious Organizations (2009)[20]

age	25–34	35–44	45–54	55–64	65–74	75 and older
% given	.80%	.89%	1.06%	1.31%	1.92%	3.22%

The bigger givers in the oldest generation are the kind whose funerals we hold each weekend in churches across the country. As that generation's $41 trillion in wealth transfers to the next generations, the church should expect to see no more than one-third of what it is accustomed to seeing, if that, according to these statistics.

Not only are the heirs less likely to be evangelical, but the heirs who are evangelical are less likely to give, to give consistently, or to give generously.

The shift away from evangelical values and beliefs grows more radical with each younger generation, as we will see in chapters 5 and 6. Those changing beliefs drive this documented decrease in giving.

Our churches and parachurches are unprepared for the 46 percent drop in donations that we will likely see in the next fourteen years. Many are already seeing a decrease as consistent and generous older givers pass away. Some ministry leaders are wondering, *What are we doing wrong?* They don't realize that, like most ministries, they are simply seeing the consequences of a national trend beyond their control.

The older generation accounts for only 19 percent of our national church, but they give 46 percent of our donations.[21] A combining of figures reveals that approximately 361,000 of these most generous American evangelicals die every year, or 989 per day.[22]

Ministry leaders at every level, from pastors of local churches to donation specialists at national parachurch ministries, know that this departing generation is the most generous, most faithful, and most capable giving generation in the American church. They are the financial core. Unfortunately, little formal research exists about the significance of these older evangelical donors— and about the failure of the younger generations to adopt these values as they age.

The Target Analytics Nonprofit Cooperative Database tracks donations from Americans. They report that each generation gives the following percent of total donations.[23]

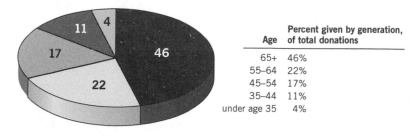

Age	Percent given by generation, of total donations
65+	46%
55–64	22%
45–54	17%
35–44	11%
under age 35	4%

By the federal government's average life expectancy, the evangelical donors who give 68 percent of evangelical budgets nationally and locally will no longer be living in twenty-four years. The donors who give about half of all evangelical gifts will die within the next fourteen years.

Experienced ministry leaders know that these generational statistics bear out in real life, but few have sat down to consider the implications. Many hope that younger evangelicals will change their lifestyles and become faithful attendees and faithful givers, but there's no evidence for such a widespread change of lifestyle and values in younger evangelicals. Few ministries have any plan for their ministry to function without 46 percent of funding in the next fifteen years.

These figures show that as the current 45- to 54-year-olds become the older generation, there will still be some vitality of giving (particularly as they inherit their parents' wealth). But unless those under age 44 change their values as they age, the evangelical juggernaut will crumble as the younger generations inherit their parents' and grandparents' $41 trillion in wealth.

This isn't surprising to ministry insiders who know the generations well. Older donors are more reliable, often remaining faithful to a church or parachurch for decades. They are more generous, giving a greater percentage of their wealth, and they generally have more wealth to give from, not only because of their age, but also because of a lifetime of choices that discouraged debt and encouraged saving.

4. The unreliability and unpredictability of ensuing generations

But haven't the oldest givers always been the most generous? In a word, yes. And the young evangelicals today will, most likely, become more generous as they age. However, that does not mean they will become as generous or consistent as the present-day older generations.

Samuel Freedman, in a New York Times story about decreasing church giving, reported:

Well before the subprime mortgage crisis threw the economy into a tailspin, warning signs for religious giving were present. A 2007 study by three professors at Indiana University-Purdue University in Indianapolis found that baby boomers in 2000 were donating about 10 percent less to religious bodies than their parents' generation did at a comparable age in 1973—and almost 25 percent less than those parents, by then ages 62 to 76, were donating in 2000.[24]

The Purdue findings are important. Here's why. We've seen that each younger generation of evangelicals is increasingly stingy. Some optimists reason that as the younger generations age, they will become more generous. And certainly, some of them will. However, the Purdue study above compares how today's older folks gave *when they were the younger folks*. It tells us that a 75-year-old giver today was, at age 35, far more generous than his 35-year-old counterpart today. Today's older generation has always been more generous than today's younger generations.

The Purdue study reports that baby boomers presently give less than their parents did *when they were the same age*. And it reports that boomers' parents also give less than their parents did *at the same age*. This is the best evidence we possess that compares the religious giving of the generations—when they were the same age. And it shows that each subsequent generation is giving less than the previous generation, even as they mature.

The generational decrease in giving from older Americans has been slow and steady. However, due to abrupt shifts in culture, the generations younger than the boomers give drastically less than our present oldest generations. Barring a radical change of course, these younger-than-boomer generations will continue giving substantially less, even when they become the oldest generations.

Responsible leaders must begin planning, not only for a decrease in overall donations, but also for instability in donations. Multiple studies show that the younger generations don't just give less, they also give less consistently.

The reliability of the older generations is demonstrated by a 2010 report about the economic recession and its drain on evangelical giving. In it, Barna Group researchers found, "Donors who were least likely to report drops in church giving included Elders (ages 65-plus)."[25]

The younger an evangelical is, the less likely he or she is to be giving at all. Younger evangelicals also give less as a percentage, from less income, and the gifts they do give are more sporadic. Lifestyle debts and negative equity also increase with younger evangelicals, further hampering the ability to give now—or when wealth is inherited.

This change is cultural, according to Villanova economics professor Charles Zech: "The so-called Greatest Generation came of age during the New Deal and World War II, developing trust in institutions. . . . The baby boomers, in contrast, learned skepticism as products of the Vietnam and Watergate years."[26]

Zech reasons that as younger American generations grow increasingly suspicious of institutions, they also grow less likely to donate to any institution, including an evangelical one. If such shifts lie beneath the generational trends, we should expect the trend of decreased giving and increased unpredictability to accelerate through the generations that follow the boomers. The younger generations are even less fond of institutions and even more egocentric than the baby boomers or even the baby busters. A similar values-change argument could be made about how much wealth each generation spends on itself.

None of these findings are particularly surprising about the upcoming generations. But again, few ministry leaders have charted any decisive or proactive path through the financial storm that has begun and will worsen over the next ten to thirty years.

A study by the Barna Group found these trends in giving:[27]

- Beyond the greatest generation givers, baby boomers are fairly generous givers, but they prefer funding parachurches, not churches. Their children, the baby busters, don't give much money at all in comparison, and prefer to give of their time, instead.
- The percentage of Americans who give at all, including tithing and supporting evangelical works, continues to decline.
- Seventeen percent of Christians say they tithe—but only 3 percent actually give 10 percent or more of their income to the Lord's work.[28]

So long as we rely on a dollar-centric ministry model, the health of our church is reduced to a by-product of the economy, the creativity of fundraisers, and the stewardship of incoming generations that have proven to be stingy, indebted, and unreliable.

Giving may seem to be the most non-spiritual and concrete of the church's present crises. In fact, it is the spiritual consequence of our failure at discipleship. Purdue economics professor Mark Ottoni-Wilhelm put it well when he said, "It's wrong to look at this as a money problem. The drop in giving follows the involvement pattern. Because people aren't as involved, the giving pattern traces it."[29] His observation tracks precisely with the trends we'll see in the next chapter, which documents the massive loss of involvement by younger evangelicals.

In a recent plea to his congregation, Robert Schuller identified the same spiritual root as the cause for the Crystal Cathedral's bankruptcy. He explained that financial survival "depends upon new people joining, making commitments, and becoming members of this ministry by their financial support."[30]

By his own account, Schuller's church failed to make new converts and failed to train its existing people into transformed living and giving. We will see, unfortunately, that the national church is broadly failing in those same two areas.

For five decades, the Crystal Cathedral has represented what is just around the corner for large evangelical churches and national ministries. Now it is financially bankrupt.

5

Bleeding

"All good-to-great companies began the process of finding
a path to greatness by confronting the brutal facts of their
current reality. . . . It is impossible to make good decisions
without infusing the entire process with an honest confronta-
tion of the brutal facts."

Jim Collins, *Good to Great*

Keep watch over yourselves and all the flock of which the Holy
Spirit has made you overseers. Be shepherds of the church of
God, which he bought with his own blood.

Acts 20:28

Scott Miller always recited his Awana Bible memory verses with
uncanny speed. The boy had a way with Scripture. He attended
Christian school and was raised by evangelical parents who have
been faithful in their thirty-five-year marriage. They took him to
church every Sunday morning. And Sunday night. And Wednesday.

Scott, now thirty, doesn't believe in God anymore. The last time
he set foot in a church building was for a wedding, two years ago. He
doesn't think the Bible is believable or reliable or relatable to his life.

Chances are, you know a Scott of your own—a young evangelical prodigal. Scott is one of about 260,000 evangelical young
people who walk away from Christianity every year. He's one of
the roughly two in three evangelical 20-somethings who abandon
the faith by age thirty.

Leaders have long reasoned that most of these kids return in their
thirties. But those who best know the demographic say that's not
the case. Scott will most likely *not* return, according to formal studies and informal expert experience with young former evangelicals.

We began this study by noting that the evangelical church is not
nearly as large as we have been told (chapter 1). Now, to honestly
assess our position, we must face another layer of brutal fact. We
are losing the people we do have. If the church is the body of Christ,
then that body is bleeding out. And it's not just our 20-somethings
who are leaving, though they're exiting faster than any other group.

This may be the most disturbing of all the trends we must face—
our failure to retain our own children as disciples. Simply keeping our own kids would hold us steady with population growth.
But we are not keeping our kids or holding our percentage in the
population.

Research indicates that more than half of those born into evangelicalism are leaving the movement during their twenties. And
the majority of them never return. This departure figure has never
been higher in the United States. The number of those who return
has never been lower.

The Lost Generation: The Statistic Nobody Wants to Face

Can it really be true, this figure that two in three young evangelicals
walk away from the faith? I'm a skeptic about simplified statistics,
so I figured this number must be an exaggeration—something
concocted by a desperate youth group fundraiser.

Until I looked into it. Until I found that in separate studies Josh
McDowell, LifeWay Research, the Barna Group, and secular researchers, including at UCLA, have all landed at figures between 69
and 80 percent of evangelicals in their twenties who leave the faith.

Josh McDowell reports that 69 percent of evangelical teens leave the church after high school.[1]

LifeWay Research found that 70 percent of Christian church attendees from the millennial generation quit attending church by age twenty-three.[2]

The LifeWay findings were so radical that Thom Rainer told *USA Today*, "The Millennial generation (those 18–29) will see churches closing as quickly as GM dealerships [this was before the government bailout]."[3] Many young pastors leading from within that generation, while thankful for notable exceptions, agree with Rainer's prediction about the larger trend.

Barna estimates that from every five young evangelicals, four will "disengage" from the church by age twenty-nine.[4]

Experts have noticed the same trend from the other side. When surveying unchurched young adult Americans, Ed Stetzer was surprised to find that the majority of unchurched young adults were previously churched, but had abandoned the church. In his book *Lost and Found*, Stetzer calls this group the *de-churched*: "We were surprised at how many of the younger unchurched indicated they had attended church as a child."[5] In fact, the "de-churched" account for the largest category of presently unchurched young people.

In a separate report Stetzer noted:

> There is no easy way to say it, but it must be said. Parents and churches are not passing on a robust Christian faith and an accompanying commitment to the church. We can take some solace in the fact that many do eventually return. But, Christian parents and churches need to ask the hard question, "What is it about our faith commitment that does not find root in the lives of our children?"[6]

Evangelical researcher David Kinnaman recently concluded, "We are at a critical point in the life of the North American church; the Christian community must rethink our effort to make disciples. Many of the assumptions on which we have built our work with young people are rooted in modern, mechanistic, and mass production paradigms.[7]

Stetzer, Barna, Rainer, McDowell, Kinnaman—the Who's Who of mainstream evangelical observers—have all noted the same undeniable trend: We are losing our young people.

"I Heard That the Young People All Return Eventually"

Many evangelical leaders have known these stats for some time, but there has been little concentrated or successful effort to fix the problem. Some leaders respond that kids will be kids. They've told each other and more than a few worried parents that most of these quitters resurface in their thirties—when divorce is crushing their marriage and their kids are driving them crazy.

Baylor University academics Rodney Stark and Byron Johnson represent this "don't panic" sentiment in a *Wall Street Journal* opinion piece titled "Religion and the Bad News Bearers." They write, "Surveys always find that younger people are less likely to attend church, yet this has never resulted in the decline of the churches. It merely reflects the fact that, having left home, many single young adults choose to sleep in on Sunday mornings."[8]

Research confirms this insight that young people are sleeping in on Sunday mornings. However, research also tells us that most of these young people will never again attend a church faithfully or consistently. And anecdotally, pastors across the country are meeting more and more former-evangelicals who are now in their early thirties. We're meeting former Christians who've had their kids, gotten their divorce, and still sleep in on Sunday mornings. They have not returned to church, and many never will. Why not? Because they don't believe in God or the Bible anymore.

The argument that kids have always left but they always return assumes that culture is fixed. It presupposes that culture and society are constant—that 20-somethings today behave the same as 20-somethings in the 1980s. That's a massive and flawed assumption in an age of rapid change. Our culture, society, and generations are changing faster than many of us can understand, let alone calculate.

As I've encountered critics who argue that we need not worry about this trend, I've noticed they all have this in common: They're old. And, in essence, they all assume that things work the same way in 2013 as they did in 1973, 1983, and 1993. But things don't still work the way they did last century.

I hope I'm wrong about the difficult news in this book. I especially hope I'm wrong about this one. And the critics who say we need not worry about this generational exodus—I hope they're right. But if the "don't cry wolf" optimists are *not* right, if these facts are, well, facts, then it's the young pastors and leaders who will live to see the decline. It's the younger generations who will be alive to see who was right—and to regret if we underestimated the difficult reality of this emigration.

Of course, some prodigals do return. As a pastor, I've counseled the stereotypical returning couple more than once. They do exist. But they are, unfortunately, the exception and not the rule. And they rarely jump back into a life of devotion, freedom, service, or giving.

Ultimately, we don't have to offer our own opinions about how many prodigals return. The professionals have done the work, and they've concluded that the majority do *not* return. LifeWay researchers have found that 35 percent of prodigals find their way back into evangelical church attendance, while 65 percent do not.[9] So roughly, of every three young evangelicals who leave, two do not return.[10]

The specialists, people who minister day and night to this demographic, are seeing that figure play out in their ministries. They affirm that the majority of prodigal evangelicals do *not* return in their thirties. The kids may have mostly returned in the 1990s, but just one in three returns nowadays.

In his book *Generation EX-Christian*, Drew Dyck answers those who would discount the trend of the lost generation:

A few recent books suggest that the bleak statistics about young people leaving the church are misleading, and that reaction to the trend has been overblown. . . . I'd love to share [that] optimism. Unfortunately, there are unique factors that I believe make this

generation different. First, young adults today are dropping their
faith at a greater rate than those of yesteryear . . . five to six times
the historic rate. . . . Comparing today's young people with their
parents may be like comparing apples and oranges.[11]

Other optimists have argued that as young people leave the
church externally, they retain the faith internally. Again, this is a
nice sentiment, but it's not true. Leaders under the age of thirty
see the emptiness of that claim, because they know these quitters
personally. These are not hypothetical people leaving the church,
and the quitters are often happy to say why they're leaving. They
don't believe anymore.

Researchers have proven this, too. After surveying three thousand United States teens and conducting thorough interviews with
250 young people, sociologists Christian Smith and Patricia Snell
concluded, "Little evidence supports the idea that emerging adults
who decline in regular external religious practice nonetheless retain over time high levels of . . . internal religious faith. Quite the
contrary is indicated by our analysis."[12]

In their own academic way, Smith and Snell say it's malarkey to
convince ourselves that all is fine internally, even as these young
people flee the church:

> Therefore, certain people interested in seeing strong religious and
> spiritual lives among emerging adults and who wish to take com-
> fort in the hope that religion remains subjectively robust for them
> even when they have dramatically reduced participating in more
> objective, public expressions of faith are not, we see, supported in
> that hope by the empirical evidence.[13]

In other words, Smith's research shows that when young people
leave on the outside, they've left on the inside, too. Are there exceptions to these trends? Of course there are, but they're just that,
exceptions. Dyck puts it this way:

> There are myriad exceptions . . . not all who leave the church leave
> the faith. There is even a minority movement of young Christians
> who have left formal church in search of a more pristine faith. But

those are the exceptions. For the vast majority, leaving the church is a decisive first step on the path away from faith. It may be comforting to view their departure as a temporary hiatus and assume that most young people will automatically return en masse. I pray that they will. Unfortunately, such thinking may do more harm than good by giving us false hope and luring us into complacency.[14]

Jeff Schadt, another specialist in this demographic, agrees. He founded and runs the Youth Transition Network, a national parachurch ministry that guides evangelical teens and 20-somethings through the college and post-college years.

Schadt has spent years traveling the nation, interviewing youth and college students in evangelical churches of all sizes and stripes. He has a knack for loosening the kids up. He jokes with them about hypocrisy in the church and guarantees them confidentiality. Then they pour out their hearts, sometimes in front of the whole youth group, about their promiscuity, feelings of not measuring up, and whatever else defines youth group and church in their mind. Schadt has been doing this for about a decade, and you wouldn't believe the stories that evangelical teens tell him.

"A lot of churches just say, 'Oh well, they'll come back later,'" Schadt says. "Not all do, and many who do return do so with broken families and serious problems, having selected their career, lifestyle and often their spouse apart from the Lord."[15] Schadt calculates that hundreds of thousands of students from youth groups and Christian schools walk away from the faith every year. And he's right.

Here are the numbers—not from Schadt—but from various other researchers. When combined, multiple studies reveal these trends in our young people.

How many 18- to 29-year-olds leave evangelical churches?

Of the 3.7 million United States evangelicals who are eighteen to twenty-nine years old, 2.6 million will leave the faith at some point between their eighteenth and twenty-ninth birthdays. That's 260,000 who leave each year. That's 712 who will quit the faith today, another 712 tomorrow, and so forth.[16]

How many return later in life?

Of the 2.6 million who leave, about 900,000 will eventually return, later in life. About 1.7 million will not return to an evangelical church, based on the evidence we have so far.

The Big Picture

If this rate of departure continues to the next generation of 18- to 29-year-olds (and the evidence indicates it will), then about 5 million people will have left the United States church between the years 2007 and 2027. That's 5 million departed from a church of about 22 million. About 3.4 million of them will never return.

The bleeding from this wound on the body of Christ is not just the red of a skinned knee. It's not a dripping cut. It's a gushing artery. We are losing almost 10 percent of our total United States evangelical church—from the generation that is most strategic to the future church.

In crude terms, these figures mean that in the last decade, some 2.6 million young evangelicals have walked away. About 1.7 million of them will never associate with a church again, and 900,000 of them will someday find their way back home. Bruised and beaten down, but home.

Keep in mind, these are conservative numbers, based on the smaller, more accurate estimated size of evangelicalism. We are losing the majority of our next generation, during their life-course-setting, formative years. Put another way, we are losing the core of the evangelical church of 2020 to 2040.

Next Christian View of God: "If He Exists, He Exists to Make Me Happy"

Then there are the findings about the kids who stay in church. Sociologist Christian Smith and researchers George Barna and David Kinnaman have independently concluded that the majority of young evangelicals are not able to articulate their faith. They belong to a faith system that depends on verbal spread of the message, but they themselves can't explain it.

If evangelical millennials cannot typically articulate the message of Jesus as Savior, then the bleed out of evangelicals may accelerate as these teens and 20-somethings age into positions of influence, parenthood, and leadership of evangelical institutions. If "faith comes from hearing" (Romans 10:17), how can the faith be passed along unless evangelicals can proclaim or explain it?

In his book *Soul Searching*, Smith writes that the common creed among American evangelical teens is "Moralistic Therapeutic Deism," which he defines as essentially a self-centered worldview, in which personal happiness is the highest goal and a distant God is taken for granted in the background. In fact, this view is so prominent that evangelical teens are no less likely than unbelievers to believe that all good people go to heaven.[17]

"Moralistic Therapeutic Deism may not simply be what an ill-informed or nominal faith sounds like in a teen interview. It may be the new mainstream American religious faith for our culturally post-Christian, individualistic, mass-consumer capitalist society," Smith writes.[18]

For his book *You Lost Me*, Kinnaman interviewed some of the strongest teenage evangelicals—those who were actively sharing their faith with unbelievers. He reports, "We found that the faith [that teen evangelists] were trying to spread was, in fact, more akin to moralistic therapeutic deism than to historic Christianity. Few of these youth evangelists could identify a single portion of the Bible as the basis of their faith in Christ."[19]

According to the Barna Group, "American teens are displaying the lowest levels of participation in prayer, reading religious resources . . . and being involved in witness to peers since Barna began surveying teenagers."[20]

The Barna Group also found this in a survey of all Americans, including but not limited to evangelicals:

> One pattern emerged loud and clear: young adults rarely possess a biblical worldview. The current study found that less than one-half of one percent of adults in the Mosaic generation—i.e., those aged

18 to 23—have a biblical worldview, compared to about one out of every nine older adults.[21]

This finding suggests sweeping implications for cultural change both inside and outside the church. Of course, if evangelical 20-somethings have not embraced a biblical worldview, then it will be difficult for them to pass on such a worldview to the next generation.

The body of Christ is bleeding out. We are losing our own kids—somehow failing to pass on a meaningful relationship with God through Jesus Christ. In Jesus' terminology, we are failing at discipleship. That is, *we are failing at the core command Jesus gave to His followers.*

This is what matters, and if these numbers are correct, we are failing at it. Jesus did not call His church to build buildings or websites or worship services. He called His followers to "make disciples."

Schadt places the blame on parents first and then on the churches that those parents support. He says many parents rely too heavily on the church to do discipleship. His research found that teens can handle and hunger for more substantial teaching than most youth groups give them.

Barna agrees: "A large majority of churched believers rely upon their church, rather than their family, to train their children to become spiritually mature."[22]

Young People Aren't the Only Ones Leaving

The body of Christ is bleeding fastest among the young. But they're not the only ones leaving.

Washington Times religion editor Julia Duin researched church exit trends for her book *Quitting Church.* She found that it's not just young people leaving. Singles over thirty-five (a growing segment of the population, due to declines in marriage and increase in divorce) and single moms of all ages are also quietly slipping out the back doors.

"My research suggested that people are simply not being pastored," Duin writes. "I ran into demographic groups, such as men and singles, who have abandoned the church in large numbers because they are fed up with their needs never being addressed. Singles are the largest demographic among the unchurched. A third group, working moms, is about to join those two demographics."[23]

These macro trends all grow out of micro failures. The church at large appears to be failing to train and nurture disciples, either through church programs or through one-on-one relationships.

For this failure, we could blame any number of factors, based on our own experiences, opinions, and theology. The culprit likely varies across ministries, but the national trend is indisputable. We are failing to disciple our people into transformed thinking or living.

Princeton professor Kenda Creasy Dean suggests that the loss of our youth is not an aberration, but an indication of what's actually going on in the larger church, among all generations. She quotes Christian Smith and Melinda Denton, who put it this way: "Most American youth faithfully mirror the aspirations, lifestyles, practices and problems of the adult world into which they are being socialized. In these ways, adolescents may actually serve as a very accurate barometer of the condition of the culture and institutions of our larger society."[24]

In all likelihood, the "problem" beneath the loss of our youth has little to do with youth, and everything to do with our fumbling of basic discipleship among our adults. As David Kinnaman writes, "The dropout problem is, at its core, a faith-development problem; to use religious language, it's a *disciple-making problem*. The church is not adequately preparing the next generation to follow Christ faithfully in a rapidly changing culture."[25]

After twenty years spent documenting the evangelical church, George Barna recently concluded, "One of the greatest frustrations of my life has been the disconnection between what our research consistently shows about churched Christians and what the Bible calls us to be."[26]

These findings align with many of our own personal experiences as evangelicals, and yet we are surprised to learn the reality that the movement is weakening and may be dying.

We are failing to make new disciples. We are losing folks from every generation. Our existing disciples are not generally reproductive in their living or transformed in their thinking. And we are losing six or seven out of every ten evangelical teens.

Somewhere along the way, our focus on programs and techniques, dollars, ministry size, and perhaps even powerful worship distracted us from the basics. Jesus did not tell Peter to build a building or a program, not a production or an organization. His words were simple, and they are the heart of the companion "solution" chapter to this trend: Healing.

> Jesus said, "Simon son of John, do you truly love me?" He answered, "Yes, Lord, you know that I love you." Jesus said, "Take care of my sheep."
>
> John 21:16

Somehow, somewhere, we have failed to take care of Christ's sheep. Now we are losing them.

6

Sputtering

Therefore go and make disciples of all nations, baptizing them in the name of the Father and of the Son and of the Holy Spirit, and teaching them to obey everything I have commanded you. And surely I am with you always, to the very end of the age.

Matthew 28:19–20

February 15, 1953. The sun was setting on the Florida coast. A swarm of 136 Oldsmobile, Buick, and Ford coupes roared and slid around the Daytona Beach Road Course. Former moonshine runner and NASCAR legend Fonty Flock held a one-minute lead over second-place driver Dick Rathmann. It was the final lap, and there seemed to be no way Flock could lose.

That's when Fonty Flock's eight-cylinder engine began sputtering. Halfway around the final lap, his motor stalled completely. As Flock's Oldsmobile coasted to a standstill—and as the crowd watched with slacked jaws—his one-minute lead disintegrated in what seemed like a few blinks of disbelief. Fonty Flock was out of gas.

On the heels of a blockbuster century, the evangelical church still seems invincible to many within the movement—and to some outsiders, too. We are the Fonty Flock of religion in the United States. In recent decades we had the power of Billy Graham, the Moral Majority, Focus on the Family, and George W. Bush. We still have Rick Warren, Tim Tebow, Christian radio, *New York Times* bestselling titles, and stadiums packed by conferences like Women of Faith and Catalyst.

But is it possible that a few big names are thriving, while the broader movement flags and fades? After all, the big names are only, to put it in courtroom terminology, circumstantial evidence.

Is it possible that our standards for success—dollars, influence, size, and fame—are not biblical measurements of the church's health? Could they be more American than biblical?

Could the actual engine of the church be sputtering? And might it soon stall out completely, even as many assume we have a one-minute lead on the competition?

The Simple Measure of Health: New Disciples

Academics and sociologists argue over exactly how to measure the success or failure of the evangelical church. But by one scriptural gauge, measuring our success or failure is embarrassingly simple.

Jesus Christ's gospel (the "evangel" from which our movement gets its name) embeds in its command to "go and make disciples" the measurement of the movement's health. By Christ's own words, this is the simplest gauge we use to measure success or failure.[1] Are we making disciples?

Not just convincing converts, but making disciples? Not just filling the seats in auditoriums, but training the souls of transformed individuals? Are we valuing the quality of our discipleship more than the quantity of our attendance?

Jesus' words and life reveal that evangel-followers can know whether they are succeeding or failing by this: whether new growing disciples are being made or not.

Of course there are a hundred other measures of health, too. But most simply, if new, reproductive disciples are being added, then a church is healthy and growing, regardless of other challenges. Jesus' command focuses on the quality, rather than the quantity of disciples. The mandate does not come with a quota, but with a clarification: "teaching them to obey everything I have commanded you" (Matthew 28:20).

When such quality disciples are being added, we are fulfilling Christ's Great Commission.[2] We see this in the lives of Jesus and His early followers, as well as in every period of church growth, from early-century Christians to current revivals in areas of China, India, and Africa. If new disciples are being trained and transformed, then the church is growing spiritually, and Jesus' commission is being fulfilled.

The opposite is just as true. If new believers are not being generated and trained, then no amount of money or political clout can right the movement. A church that isn't making disciples is—at that moment—a declining, dying, or failing church. At the very least, its engine is stalled.

Let's not forget, a politically powerful and financially flush church that failed to make disciples resulted in the near death of evangelicalism during the thus-named Dark Ages. Scripture and history both argue that the engine of evangelicalism is new conversions. They are the litmus of church health, demonstrated time and again in the last two thousand years.

Legitimate converts will spread the evangel (or gospel message of salvation in Jesus Christ), regardless of political or financial means, or even formal training. On the other hand, political and financial means—without radical converts—result in religion that is either reproductively impotent (as with Western Europe and many United States mainline denominations) or not about the evangel (as with the Roman Church), regardless of resources.

Ironically, many of the factors that we consider signs of health in the contemporary United States church are actually signs of wealth and power—things that have nothing to do with Christ's mandate. For example, we are almost universally guilty of looking to the "mighty reach"—shining facilities and multimillion dollar budgets of our parachurch and megachurch ministries—and concluding that the movement must be thriving.

Our wealth and facilities may give the appearance of a healthy and thriving church—just as the new homes and rocketing equity of the early 2000s gave the appearance of great economic health in the United States, and just as Fonty Flock's one-minute lead gave the appearance of certain victory.

But let's look deeper. In the United States, how is the condition of our spiritual engine, the true motor of the church? How are we doing at making disciples who remain? Is our engine revving, or has it stalled?

The United States Evangelical Population Is Slowly Declining—Even as the United States Population Rapidly Surges

After fifty years of financially flush, ever-expanding evangelical organizations, the number of evangelical disciples in the United States has decreased as a percentage of the population.[3] In the following research we will see that each ensuing generation of Americans has fewer evangelicals than the previous generation. By this most basic measure, the engine of evangelicalism is not roaring. It's barely sputtering.

We have seen that the broad evangelical church is smaller than we thought (Inflated). We've seen that this smaller church is bleeding out—losing our own kids (Bleeding). Now we'll confront a number of studies that reveal the engine of disciple-making is not turning fast enough to keep pace with population growth.

We don't hear about it on the news, but the United States is presently undergoing a population boom that outpaces the explosion of the 1950s' baby boom. George Barna reports:

> The country has had more than four million births each year since 2000—the first time we've hit the four million mark since 1993. In fact, in 2007 we set a record for births (4.317 million), eclipsing the record set in 1957 during the Baby Boom era. . . . That radical increase in births does not include immigration, which adds another 1 million new United States residents each year.[4]

Between the new baby boom and the immigrant boom, the United States population is rocketing. Unfortunately, the national evangelical church is not. Despite the exciting things we see at some exceptional churches, our national church numbers are not keeping pace with population growth.

As a percentage of the population, evangelicalism is shrinking in the United States.[5] When larger state and national numbers are considered, a significant percentage of the "growth" that evangelical churches claim is merely transfer from other churches or denominations. Julia Duin, religion editor of the *Washington Times*, put this well: "Much church growth is due to transfers from one church to another."[6]

Research indicates that even the states with the largest, seemingly healthiest, and nationally modeled church movements—California, Texas, and Florida, for example—are among the many states where evangelicalism saw no net growth, but rather a net decline in recent years.

Evangelicalism Is Shrinking, While Secularism Is Soaring

Evangelicalism, like all types of Christianity, is dying in the United States, according to the Pew Forum on Religion and Public Life's most recent United States Religious Landscape Survey. And the blood is spilling fastest from the younger generations. As the Pew study conservatively states, "If these generational patterns persist, recent declines in the number of Protestants and growth in the size of the unaffiliated population may continue."[7]

As the U.S. church shrinks, the number of nonreligious and secular Americans is skyrocketing. If you took a group of one hundred evangelicals today, there would be a corresponding group of two hundred overtly secular nonbelievers. The two hundred overt secularists include stated atheists, agnostics, and the non-religious. More significant than the outnumbering is the breakdown by age. The percentage of evangelicals decreases with each younger generation, while the percentage of agnostics and atheists increases in younger generations. The net effect over time will be a tsunami-like culture shift, as the older generations pass away.

The Pew's age-by-religion findings reveal that the evangelical church is top-heavy. That is, 45 percent of evangelicals will die within the next twenty-nine years[8]—meaning that evangelicals in the population could drop from about 7 percent of Americans now to about 4 percent or less—unless new disciples are generated.

The reduced influence of evangelicals will take another steep drop after the passing of the boomers—the last generation that makes up as great a percentage in the church as it does in the population.

With each younger generation, evangelicals account for less of their generation. For example, folks age sixty-five and older account for 16 percent of the United States population, but they account for 19 percent of the evangelical church. Here are the findings:

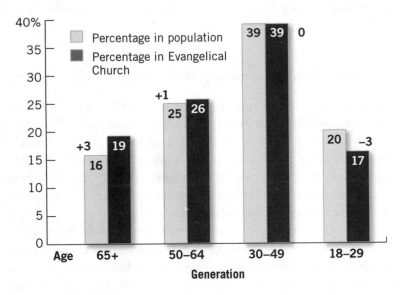

Note the trend of decreasing percentage within the church, compared to population, as the generations get younger.

What does this chart mean? It means that if you took one hundred people from the population, sixteen would be older than sixty-five. But if you took one hundred people from the evangelical church, nineteen would be older than sixty-five. And while twenty of every one hundred from the population are ages eighteen to twenty-nine, only seventeen in the church's one hundred are ages eighteen to twenty-nine. *It means that with each passing generation, evangelicalism is shrinking. The church is top-heavy in age.*[9] The trend is subtle, but it shows that evangelicals, as a percentage of their generations, are consistently decreasing.

Quite simply, with each ensuing generation of Americans, fewer are evangelical Christians—*not more and not even the same.*

Even more revealing is the opposite trend among those who self-identified as "atheist." It's a radical *increase* among the younger:

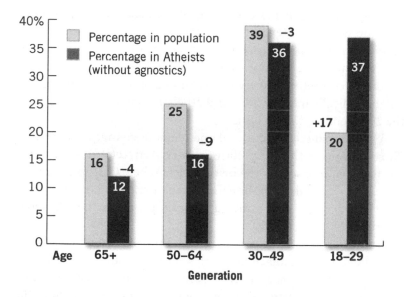

Note the radical increase in the youngest generation. The steady generational decrease of evangelicals is mirrored by an aggressive increase among stated atheists. Evangelicals—already outnumbered two to one by secularists—are primarily gray hairs. Atheists are mostly in their prime. The numbers for agnostics and other secularists parallel those of the atheists.

Also, note that for 18- to 29-year-olds, there are twice as many atheists as evangelicals, by generation, within each belief. So, while there may be one evangelical for every two overt secularists now, the ratio will increase rapidly in the next twenty-nine years, as older evangelicals pass away and as secularists continue to account for more of the upcoming generations.

From the generation of 18- to 29-year-olds, there are roughly four to six secularists (atheists, agnostics, and self-identified non-believers combined) for every one evangelical.[10] If the trend of decrease in the church and increase in secularism continues, it's not farfetched to expect the United States to be as secular as England or Germany within a matter of decades. The weight of evangelicalism will die off, just as the weight of a new secular society hits.

More precisely, as the percentage of evangelicals is slowly decreasing with each generation, atheism and agnosticism are aggressively *increasing* in each younger generation.

If the same bleed out of evangelicals and acceleration of secularization continues, society in the United States of 2030 or 2040 will be radically more secular and atheistic than many children of the 20th century can imagine.

A similar tsunami of cultural and religious change transformed Great Britain in the early 20th century. Artifacts of a formerly Christian culture scatter the British Isles. Where Glasgow's motto once read "Let Glasgow flourish by the preaching of the Word and the praising of His name," it now simply reads "Let Glasgow flourish."[11]

Home to some of the world's oldest Protestant seminaries and cathedrals, and birthplace to Charles Dickens, Spurgeon, and C. S. Lewis, Britain is now an overtly secular nation. Christianity has so waned and left such a spiritual vacuum that the most common name for newborn boys in Britain is now Mohammed,[12] and some preachers are arrested for stating that homosexuality is a sin.[13]

The United States of the early 2000s is in many ways different from the Britain of the early 1900s, but it is also on the same trajectory of evangelical recession. The loss of the incoming generations and the rapid acceleration of secular society are the most obvious parallels. Darwin shook the Christian moorings of Great Britain in the 1860s. By 1920 the country had clearly abandoned Christianity.

Similarly, the 1960s in the United States were marked by a secular shift—the removal of prayer from schools, the push for legalized abortions, and a last turning of the corner for Darwinist teaching in United States schools and society at large. If that parallel pattern continues, the 2020s may mark the same final abandoning of Christianity in the United States.

At the present rate of cultural change, Americans in twenty years may be as unaware of Billy Graham and the once-powerful religious right as they are now unaware of tent revivals, D. L. Moody, and Prohibition.

Biggest Loser: Geographically, Even the Bright Spots of Evangelicalism Are Losing

So, what about the bright spots of evangelicalism? Aren't there exceptions to this trend in the United States? There are certainly exceptional churches, leaders, and ministries. However, national church statisticians haven't found states or regions with enough exceptional churches to make up the difference for the decline. When we zoom out to a national or state-by-state view, even the beacons of evangelical hope turn out to be dimming.

Take for example the growing evangelical church in your community. It may be an exception, but the national trend is that the growing church in an area is mostly attracting transfer sheep from other smaller and struggling churches.[14]

Let's take the scenario of two hundred people leaving Church A. Let's say 150 of them go to the growing Church B in town, while another fifty of them drop out. The "growth" of 150 at Church B seems like real kingdom growth to everybody who worships there. What we are seeing is not an expansion of the evangelical church. Actually, if the other fifty from Church A never do find a church home and eventually wander spiritually, it is a loss.

Incidentally, more than half of evangelicals now attend these larger growing churches, which continue to absorb folks from smaller churches. As a result, most of us have the perception that "the church" is growing.[15] Unfortunately, perception is often not reality. In this case, reality is counterintuitive to our common perceptions.

We know this because there's an organization that tracks the total attendance at *all* evangelical churches. David Olson revealed his findings in the book *The American Church in Crisis* (Zondervan, 2008). It is the result of years surveying more than 200,000 United States churches, to identify actual growth or loss trends.

Below I have compared Olson's findings to population growth figures. The combination reveals a consistent decrease in evangelical churches, as a percentage of the population. The trend from 2000 to 2005 in most states was a decrease in attendance at evangelical churches, even as the population grew in almost all those states.[16] The states with the largest and apparently healthiest churches and ministries—some of which are modeled nationally—all saw a net decrease in attendance at evangelical churches.

California—home of Saddleback, dozens of megachurches, and radio teachers like Greg Laurie, John MacArthur, and Chuck Smith—lost 1.8 percent of its evangelical attendees between 2000 and 2005.[17] During the same time the state population actually increased by 1.3 percent, for a 3.1 percent total decrease in percent of the population attending an evangelical church.[18]

Texas—home to dozens of megachurches and national ministries, including Dallas Theological Seminary, Joel Osteen, Max Lucado, Chuck Swindoll, and others—lost 2.6 percent of its evangelical church attendees,[19] even as the population grew by about 2 percent, a nearly 5 percent swing.[20]

The same trend afflicted the entire Bible-Belt region, including evangelical powerhouse states like Georgia, home to Andy Stanley's congregations, and Florida.

Arizona is an example of apparent growth. From 2000 to 2005, attendance at evangelical churches in Arizona increased by 1.5 percent, but it did not actually keep pace with a population growth of 3.5 percent.[21]

Religion reporter Christine Wicker summarizes the evangelical church's struggling engine this way: "Evangelicals are not converting and cannot convert non-Christian adult Americans, especially native-born white people, in significant numbers."[22]

I would clarify that we are converting non-Christian adults—but not fast enough to maintain our percentage in a rapidly growing population. We are falling behind.

These trends aren't so shocking when we examine the lives of typical evangelicals around us. How many brand-new Christian converts have you met in the last year? Compare that to the number of births every day at the closest local hospital. Of the new members introduced to your congregation (if your congregation still introduces members), how many met Jesus as Savior for the first time, there at your church? How many were already believers when they began attending?

In 2011, *Christianity Today* reporter Sarah Pulliam Bailey asked Billy Graham, "What are the most important issues facing evangelicals today?" Graham's answer:

> The most important issue we face today is the same the church has faced in every century: Will we reach our world for Christ? In other words, will we give priority to Christ's command to go into all the world and preach the gospel? Or will we turn increasingly inward, caught up in our own internal affairs or controversies, or simply becoming more and more comfortable with the status quo? Will we become inner-directed or outer-directed? The central issues of our time aren't economic or political or social, important as these are. The central issues of our time are moral and spiritual in nature, and our calling is to declare Christ's forgiveness and hope and transforming power to a world that does not know him or follow him. May we never forget this.[23]

George Barna has found this about the United States evangelical church: "At any given time, a majority of believers do not have a specific person in mind for whom they are praying in the hope that the person will be saved. . . . Most churched Christians believe that since they are not gifted in evangelism, such outreach is not a significant responsibility of theirs."[24]

For his book *The Shape of Faith to Come*, Brad Waggoner surveyed 2,500 Protestant churchgoers of all ages. He found, "In the past six months, only 29 percent said that they had shared with someone how to become a Christian twice or more, and 57 percent said they had not done so at all."[25]

In his parting command, Jesus gave us the most concrete measure of spiritual success. We have, for the most part, explained it away. We are not successfully inviting folks into our movement, and yet, we are surprised it is shrinking.

Part Two

Six Solutions for Recovery

7

Re-Valuing

How to Become 21st-Century Evangelicals

"Christianity has died many times and risen again; for it had
a God who knew the way out of the grave."

G. K. Chesterton, *The Everlasting Man*

Have you ever kicked yourself for not acting on good advice? Before home values took a nationwide dive, I was advised to sell a property I owned. But I failed to act.

In 2005, I bought a Scottsdale, Arizona, condo for $120,000. Two years later, the property had gained about $100,000 in value. Around that time, a billionaire Arizona land tycoon told me I should sell. I thought he was probably right, but I didn't act on his advice. Later, when prices began falling, I still neglected to take action and sell.

I never doubted the expert was correct about values going down, but I doubted the drop would be as drastic or as rapid as it turned out to be. My thought was along these lines: *Sure, the property might lose the $100,000 it has appreciated, but it probably won't drop below the price I paid for it.*

As it turns out, like most of the country, I underestimated the speed and severity of the disaster. And the expert was right. Five years after I was advised to sell for about $240,000, the property sold for $48,900.

I lost a lot, because I failed to act. I was warned, and I even agreed with the gist of the warning. But I didn't act because it would have been uncomfortable. In retrospect, acting on the advice was the furthest thing from risky, but in the moment, action felt risky.

Similarly, some will agree with the trends we've seen. They'll agree, but they'll fail to act. They won't make the difficult decisions needed to change course and avert disaster. Those leaders and their ministries will lose a lot. They will be surprised by the speed and severity of the disaster—the drastic and rapid changes brought by the Great Evangelical Recession. Their ministries will pay a great price because they lack the courage to act.

Change is risky. Action is risky. But failing to act is even riskier. Knowing these trends will not change the future of our ministries. If we hope to salvage God's work in the United States, we must choose to act on our knowledge.

All We've Learned Is No Help If We Don't Act on It

It takes great resolve and moral energy to be proactive and strategic rather than reactive and manic. Changing the course of our ministries will be difficult. It will be misunderstood. It will be demanding. But times of crisis require leaders to lead.

The evangelical mission agencies, colleges, radio stations, humanitarian nonprofits, churches, and seminaries that simply react to 21st-century trends will find themselves behind the curve—responding far too slowly to a world that's changing far too quickly. They'll follow in the decline of Borders, Blockbuster, and established newspapers—all of which seemed invincible just years before their bankruptcies.

Conversely, the ministries that humbly accept where they are—and apply God's truth to these trends—can be ahead of the curve in the 21st century. They can be less surprised and more prepared.

For many, such preparations will be the difference between closing the doors and thriving in the next thirty years.

George Barna has written this about the future of the evangelical church: "The changes that so many lament today will give rise to a more nimble, alert, discerning, and adventurous church. . . . Shifting from the known to the unknown is always uncomfortable, but intelligent and responsive changes will birth a church better able to minister effectively in the new millennium."[1]

Aware of the need for proactive, strategic change, we now shift gears. From researching to planning. From observing to preparing. From absorbing facts to prayerfully leading.

United States evangelicalism will not radically change overnight. But it will change faster than we expect—whether we want it to or not. If the first decade of the 21st century has taught us anything, it's proven that massive industries can die, ignite, or turn course with stunning speed.

The trending direction of the national evangelical church is clear. Like the value of my old Scottsdale condo, it has peaked and is now declining. We may still enjoy a season where we can shrug off our losses and keep the lights on with our 20th-century techniques and paradigms. But the fraying edges are beginning to show. The evangelical market—for lack of a better term—has begun its drop. And the accelerating decline will, in time, become an obvious dive. At that point, disagreeing or pointing fingers won't solve any problems. At that point, it will be too late to act on the knowledge conveyed in this book. All we've learned is no help if we don't act on it.

All We've Learned Is Depressing If We Don't Turn to God About It

> You don't minister to a dying nation without feeling the death pangs in yourself.
>
> Charles R. Swindoll, in a sermon on Jeremiah

We have seen that the United States church is smaller than we thought. She is bleeding, sputtering, and bankrupt. She is hated by the world, and she is dividing herself. If you're not discouraged by now, maybe you've just been skimming. Or maybe you've lost sight of the eternal and global stakes at play in this spiritual struggle.

The trends that we've tracked in such sterile terms speak to a tangible death-or-life battle between the unseen forces of evil and good. The scene is not as small as our ministries or even the patchwork of ministries based in the United States. The scene is the lurching advance of darkness, stomping and pounding as it invades the territories of light.

The stakes are eternal.

The victims or victors are not our organizations or churches, but souls that will live forever. This is the spiritual landscape. And against such a red sky, under the charred backdrop of such ominous clouds, we see these trends, not merely as observations about a cultural recession, but as stonewalls through which enemy forces have broken. These declines are crumbling gates. A torrent of armed forces is invading through these collapsed defenses—stealing our children, destroying our wealth, and dividing our people against each other.

Looking back on such a craggy horizon, the sun setting in a bloodred sky of pessimism, we can feel a bit like Frodo the hobbit in *The Lord of the Rings*. We are tiny creatures entrusted with an impossible task—to rescue humanity from unthinkable evil.

At this point in our journey, I think of the moment when a discouraged and distraught Frodo looks to the Christ-figure, Gandalf, and whimpers, "I wish the Ring had never come to me. I wish none of this had happened." To which Gandalf replies, "So do all who live to see such times; but that is not for them to decide. All we have to decide is what to do with the time that is given to us. There are other forces at work in this world. . . ."

Indeed, there are great spiritual forces at work in human history. With every country and continent and culture at His bidding, God placed you and me precisely here at the start of the 21st century. He positioned us with influence in the wealthiest church in history. He planted us at the epicenter of a global communications explosion. God has eternal purposes that hinge on your strategic placement here in the United States "for such a time as this."

Like little Frodo, we may wish *not* to know what we have learned about Christ's church in the United States. We may wish *not* to be the ones called to carry such a responsibility—not at such a crucial juncture in church history. We may wish to close our eyes to the evil encircling our nation and dividing our weakening church. Couldn't there be better servants and leaders for this moment?

When our hearts grasp the magnitude of these trends, we see that we are tiny, insufficient creatures, entrusted with a task of severe and eternal importance.

In the previous chapters we have pulled back the skin. We have examined the ripped and rotting condition of our church's internal injuries. It has been discouraging work, and if we're not careful, it can turn our attention away from our King and toward our own weakness.

When Paul found himself at a tipping point of self-weakness in ministry, God gave him these words: "My grace is sufficient for you, for my power is made perfect in weakness" (2 Corinthians 12:9).

Paul's incredible success did not come from Paul's strength. It came from his weakness—a conduit for God's strength. When describing his labors, Paul wrote that it was not *his* strength moving his weary hands and heart. No, he served, "struggling with all [God's] energy, which so powerfully works in me" (Colossians 1:29).

Weakness opens the way for God's power. Paul knew the power for Christ's church did not spring from himself. In fact, the tentmaker was so acquainted with God's strength in him, that he saw his many weaknesses as opportunities—leaking rips in the canvas, through which all of God's power could rush in, in overwhelming currents. Paul came to understand that God's grace and power best entered his life when they entered through the rips in the fabric of his pride and self-sufficiency.

And so, when Paul stared down the demons of discouragement, he could say, "Therefore I will boast all the more gladly about my weaknesses, so that Christ's power may rest on me. That is why, for Christ's sake, I delight in weaknesses, in insults, in hardships, in persecutions, in difficulties. For when I am weak, then I am strong" (2 Corinthians 12:9–10).

We have now seen our weaknesses. We have seen the rips in the fabric of the United States church—actual realities that some with good intentions will explain away, because they fear the appearance of weakness. But Paul didn't fear weakness. He delighted in it. He never based his hope for the church in the trajectory of the church. He always based his hope for the church in Christ.

Rather than explaining these realities away or ignoring them because they're uncomfortable, let us pray Paul's prayer for ourselves and for our church. Let us pray that in our weakness, in insults, in hardships, in persecutions, in difficulties, Jesus Christ might be strong. For His power is made perfect not in the strong, not in those who think that nothing is wrong, but in the weak, and in those aware of their weakness.

- We do well to acknowledge that we are weak, as a national church.
- We do well to see that we do not have it figured out.
- We do well to accept the rips in the fabric of evangelicalism.
- We do well to swallow the thick truth that many of our best efforts are not only failing, but actually backfiring.
- We do well to see our weakness, so that we can come to Him who invites the weary and burdened to fall into His arms. Jesus' invitation for tired laborers applies to us: "Come to me, all who are tired from carrying heavy loads, and I will give you rest" (Matthew 11:28 GW).

Who carries a heavier load? Who is more tired these days than faithful evangelical leaders and servants? We carry a massive, fraying, struggling, and ofttimes kicking and biting church. We open our arms to a culture that either ignores or strikes us.

As we move from observations to answers, I invite you to set this book down and kneel at intervals. I invite you to come with me to Jesus, to shed tears on these pages, for Christ's betrothed. To weep over our own inadequacy. To exchange our weakness for His strength. To exchange our agenda for His.

His strength can rush into our movement, through the rips in our fabric. Will you be weak enough to humble yourself with me, in the next stage of our journey? Will you, as the Spirit leads, kneel with me on our too-soft, uncalloused knees, and pray that the God of the nations will have mercy on us, on our children, and on our church?

Will you join me in praying this not only for the national church and its leaders, but for yourself, for your own ministry and city? Will you be weak with me? And will you lead from weakness, as Paul did, so that Christ might be strong?

We are in desperate need to see God's strength again.

The Strength of the 21st-Century Church and of the 1st-Century Church

Walk with me to the rough-hewn door of a 1st-century Jerusalem home. Eavesdrop on the worries, the prayers, and fears of Christ's followers there. Every single evangelical Christian in the world—gathered in one room—numbering not in the millions. Not in the thousands. Not in the hundreds. But a very humble, weak, and discouraged 120 Christians.

Let's return there. Let's be among them. And let's believe. God used this small group to ignite a millennial flame and catch nations ablaze. That God is still alive and working today. He is still moving and breathing today. He is, even when we forget, the head of His church in the United States. He has plans for His church here, if we will set our perceived strength aside, if we will be weak enough to let Him work through us.

The Holy Spirit and His "power" run like steel trusses under the church in Acts. We see them paired in the profound promise of Acts 1:8: "But you will receive *power* when the *Holy Spirit* comes on you; and you will be my witnesses."

God knew His 120 followers would need power to be His witnesses, so He gave them His Holy Spirit.

God knows His 20-some million followers in the United States need power to be His witnesses, so He gives us His Holy Spirit.

Plenty of New Testament professors have said the book of Acts is not so much "the acts of the apostles" as it is "the acts of the Holy Spirit." And in Acts 9:31, God testifies to this:

> Then the church throughout Judea, Galilee and Samaria enjoyed a time of peace. It was strengthened; and encouraged by the Holy Spirit, it grew in numbers, living in the fear of the Lord.

It was not Paul or Peter who strengthened, encouraged, and grew the church. It was the Holy Spirit. How many *other* things have we hoped might "strengthen," "encourage," or build our church "in number"? How many strategies? How many personalities? How many conferences?

As the great missionary J. Hudson Taylor observed, "We have given too much attention to methods and to machinery and to resources, and too little to the Source of power, the filling with the Holy Ghost."

The same Spirit who empowered the 1st-century church waits today to empower the 21st-century church in the United States. We may have neglected God's Spirit and His power, but they have not neglected us, and they will never abandon us.

The same power-breathing Holy Spirit spoke God's Scriptures into our hearts and hands (2 Timothy 3:16). And so, as we shift gears to discover solutions to our problems, we will not be looking to human experts for answers. We'll be looking to God's Word, to see God's plans and God's solutions for His church in the United States.

Margaret Feinberg had it right when she said:

> More than anything, the church is very, very tired—so many new programs, initiatives, and events. In that place of exhaustion, we don't need the latest program or initiative as much as we need people who are falling in love with God and the Scriptures.[2]

In the following chapters we'll ask God to draw us deeper into *His* plan for *His* church. As we pray for our individual ministries and our national movement, we'll look to the eternal *Word* of God. We'll look with the help of the *Spirit* of God, with the hope of changing the *people* of God.

Jesus promised He would build His church, and "the gates of hell will not prevail against it." The six forces I've documented will cripple the evangelical church *as we know it*, but they do not stand in the way of Christ's kingdom. Ministries and leaders who anticipate these forces, who align with Scripture and pray strategically, can be innovators. Ministries and leaders who cry out for rescue and redirection will be guided by the same God who guided Moses, David, Peter, and Paul.

Unfortunately, ministries that ignore these trends—and their speed—may soon become the first victims of the evangelical recession.

The following chapters prepare you and your ministry for spiritual success as 21st-Century Evangelicals.[3] Each chapter suggests biblical solutions to address the declines documented in the church. Together, they deliver a fresh call to biblical leadership:

- A call to rediscover our ambassadorship to a foreign culture (Good)
- A call to renew evangelical unity (Uniting)
- A call to redefine ministry funding (Solvent)
- A call to rebirth discipleship and shepherding (Healing)
- A call to resurrect personal evangelism (Re-Igniting)

We'll learn how to recession-proof our ministries. We'll learn how to reverse these negative national trends, by returning to God's plan for His church. These solutions don't require any one American church model. They can work in Reformed churches and purpose-driven churches, in missional churches and denominational churches. These solutions can be implemented in congregations of all sizes, from thirty to thirty thousand.

Now that you know the true footing of the United States church, don't fail to act on what you've learned. Don't fail to lead now. The next phase of our journey will require brutal self-assessment of our ministries and ourselves. Don't allow pride or busyness to eclipse the work that God will do—if we will be weak before Him.

A. W. Tozer summarized well the second half of our journey.

It will cost something to walk slow in the parade of the ages, while excited men of time rush about confusing motion with progress. But it will pay in the long run, and the true Christian is not much interested in anything short of that.[4]

8

Good

How to Conduct Ourselves in a Hostile Host Culture

Live such *good* lives among the pagans that, though they accuse you of doing wrong, they may see your *good* deeds and glorify God. . . . For it is God's will that by doing *good* you should silence the ignorant talk of foolish men.

1 Peter 2:12, 15

Steph B. knows bad people. And she knows good people, too. Steph knows how it feels to be bought and sold, to be beaten and raped. When she was a teenager, Steph's pimp prostituted her in Phoenix, Arizona, selling her body to anyone who wanted to use it. Like many sexually exploited children, Steph had no way, physically or emotionally, of escaping the slavery of sexual trafficking.

Statistically, Steph was on course to die by age thirty from drug overdose, STD-related illness, or murder (prostitutes have the highest murder rate in the United States, due to paid rapes gone too far).

"I never even saw myself making it past age eighteen," she says. That's when she was rescued, at age eighteen. Steph says this of the Christian counselor who walked alongside her in her recovery from the bondage of sex trafficking:

> She has brought light into the darkest places of my heart by loving me unconditionally. For seven or eight months she just loved me and invested in me, and never pushed me spiritually. It was through that love that I received from her that I've really been a lot more accepting of the church. Even a year ago I was really anti-church. Now I'm not a Christian, but I'm a lot more accepting of it and open to it. That's because she showed me love and was very conscious of my own needs and my own spiritual abuse.[1]

Some of Steph's abusers claimed to be Christians, so her spiritual wounds are deep and legitimate. Despite those wounds, Steph now knows evangelicals can be good people. She knows this because her counselor and friend, Celestia Tracy, has been so undeniably *good*. Celestia and her husband, Dr. Steve Tracy, sacrificed themselves to show relentless love to Steph. Their team at Mending the Soul Ministries restores victims of sex trafficking. Together, they have trained hundreds of counselors and mentors to show God's *good*ness to abuse victims, through sensitive and informed biblical counseling.

The Tracys are two among thousands of evangelicals who actively go into the dark places of United States culture—injecting God's redemption into human tragedy. This is, according to the New Testament, how we respond to an aggressive and hostile host culture—by taking God's goodness straight into the darkness.

As segments of the United States culture grow hostile and hateful toward Bible-believing Christians, we must take care to be proactive, as Christ was. If we're not intentional, we will be reactive, falling into defensive or oppositional positions. History has taught us that such reactionism to the culture only isolates us and minimizes our impact for Christ.

How does God tell us to respond when the culture turns hostile toward us? He tells us to actively live such "good" lives among the pagans that those who hate us cannot deny we are busy doing a lot of "good" (see 1 Peter 2:12, 15).

The United States is sprinting into the 21st century, and we evangelicals find ourselves surrounded by various new and strange tribes of Americans. Though the majority of these tribes speak English, many of them are radically foreign to us in their beliefs, assumptions, values, morality, and use of language. Increasingly, these tribes hate and antagonize us.

When we send missionaries to foreign tribes in Africa or New Guinea, we don't expect those tribes to immediately embrace evangelical values. We understand the missionary must first demonstrate love, show God's goodness, build relationships, learn the language, and invest in individuals and leaders. We expect that the missionary will be misunderstood and likely hated or suspected.

Successful evangelicals will learn to take the same biblical approach to the foreign tribes now growing in the United States. For too long we have expected United States nonbelievers to behave and believe like Christians. When they have acted like pagans, we have at times attacked them for being precisely who they are apart from Christ. This has brought us into distracting conflict with a number of United States tribes, including the broad tribe of Americans who self-identify as homosexual.

As documented in chapter 2 (Hated), evangelicals are on a crash course with the homosexual people group—due to tectonic shifts in cultural assumptions and values. We have also fed this conflict with evangelical reactionism, oppositionalism, and at times, outright prejudice. It is a fact that evangelicals are viewed in the broader United States culture as hateful and bigoted toward homosexuals. *How tragic that we are seen as hating the very people God commands us to love.* So how would God have us show His goodness to this tribe? How would God have you and me show His goodness to the gay men and women in each of our lives?

First, we should prepare ourselves, knowing that we *will* be misunderstood and slandered by people from other tribes in the United States. Christopher Yuan is a formerly gay, HIV-positive evangelical professor and speaker. In 2011 the Yale Christian Fellowship and Yale Students for Christ invited Yuan to speak to them. Their intent was to learn how to be more sensitive to lesbian, gay, bisexual, and transgender students on their campus.

Unfortunately, when word of Yuan's visit traveled around campus, the Christian groups' motives were overlooked in a firestorm of conflict. The Christian groups and Yuan himself were accused of hatred and bigotry—before they could even explain their motives or message.

The *Yale Daily News* documented the uproar in a story titled "Controversial Minister Draws Outcry." Reader comments under the story included "To Mr. Yuan: Do you believe homosexual men should be killed, as the Bible commands? See Leviticus 20:13."[2]

When the Christian groups published a sensitive letter titled "Why We Invited Christopher Yuan," comments under the letter included "Being a friendly bigot doesn't undo the bigotry" and "They were abhorrent people, but they have a right to a speech. . . . Mind you, I'm offended by this wahoo w[a]ndering around selling his ex-gay stuff."[3]

These comments demonstrate the cultural divide between some thought tribes at Yale and well-meaning evangelicals. Here's another insightful comment:

> No matter how many times you use the word "love," when you proclaim the LGBTQ community sinful, and when you openly call for them to spend their entire lives celibate rather than engaging in the search for love and family that makes us human, you are still doing grave harm to that community. Invoking "God's love" is not a get-out-of-jail-free card. As you said, you are not perfect. A truly loving God would be disappointed in Yuan and his message.[4]

Yuan's topic is inescapably controversial, but he is sensitive in his delivery. Given his history as a homosexual, he exercises caution. Nonetheless, the Yale student who coordinates reservations in the hall where Yuan was scheduled to speak canceled his reservation. She told the *Yale Daily News* she did so because Yuan brings a message "of bigotry and hatred."[5]

There's a tragic irony that Yale was founded in 1701 as a seminary for Bible study and that many Yale students would now forbid a speaker to explain a biblical interpretation of a contemporary issue. Conversely, Yale now holds an annual Sex Week on campus, complete with live demonstrations of sex toys.

These are not just college students expressing distaste for Bible-believing Christianity. These are the Ivy League men and women aimed at positions of prominence in making and enforcing the laws and values of United States culture. The tone during the conflict over Yuan's visit was not a tone of fairness or intellectual curiosity, but of outright hate toward a man who was gay and is HIV-positive. Why the hate? Because he is now an evangelical and now sensitively holds a biblical view about sexuality.

Each of us will encounter this same sort of hate in the coming years and decades. Many of the tribespeople who antagonize evangelicals believe—in their worldview—they are doing the loving thing for the persecuted people of their day, by putting evangelical "bigots" in their place.

Such unfair accusations can roil our human defensiveness. It's instinctive to protect ourselves, stand up for our rights, and demand fair or reasonable treatment. But we didn't typically see Jesus do this when he was misunderstood.

So how do we silence unfair accusations hurled against us? Let's start with Scripture. Living in a pagan and hypersexual culture may be new and frightening to us, but it was the norm for New Testament churches. Homosexuality and hypersexuality were nothing new to New Testament cultures or Christians. Time and again, God repeats His strategy: Live "good" lives *among* pagans.

Do not repay evil with evil or insult with insult, but with blessing. . . . Who is going to harm you if you are eager to do *good*? . . . Do this with gentleness and respect, keeping a clear conscience, so that those who speak maliciously against your good behavior in Christ may be ashamed of their slander. It is better, if it is God's will, to suffer for doing *good* than for doing evil.

1 Peter 3:9–17

Remind the people to be subject to rulers and authorities, to be obedient, to be ready to *do whatever is good*. . . . I want you to stress these things, so that those who have trusted in God may *be careful to devote themselves to doing what is good*. . . . Our people must learn to *devote themselves to doing what is good*.

Titus 3:1, 8, 14

Do not be overcome by evil, but *overcome evil with good*.

Romans 12:21

Let us not become weary in *doing good*, for at the proper time we will reap a harvest if we do not give up. Therefore, as we have opportunity, *let us do good to all people*.

Galatians 6:9–10

And God is able to make all grace abound to you, so that in all things at all times, having all that you need, *you will abound in every good work*.

2 Corinthians 9:8

And let us consider how we may spur one another on toward love and *good* deeds.

Hebrews 10:24

For it is by grace you have been saved. . . . For we are God's workmanship, *created in Christ Jesus to do good works*, which God prepared in advance for us to do.

Ephesians 2:8, 10

Command them to *do good*, to *be rich in good deeds*, and to be generous and willing to share.

1 Timothy 6:18

"In the same way, let your light shine before men, *that they may see your good deeds* and praise your Father in heaven."

Matthew 5:16

How do we silence unfair accusations hurled against us? Answer: by our good deeds (1 Peter 2:15). Unfortunately, we have hidden most of our good deeds under the bushel. I speak of the old children's song, "Hide it under a bushel? No!"

Jesus said that our "good deeds" will praise our Father in heaven (Matthew 5:16), but not if we hide our good deeds under a bowl, or bushel. It has not been our intent, but so many of our good deeds take place within the bushels of our churches, or they take place on other continents. Many of the "pagans" living on our same streets in the United States don't ever see our good deeds. Instead, they see our absence, or worse, our defensive reactions to the changing United States culture. They see our antagonism against their tribe, against *them*. We give the impression of insecurity, self-protectiveness, and hate on the outside, even as we secretly conduct good deeds in the safety and shade of the bushel.

On accident, we have huddled under the bushel. We have hidden the light of the world from some of the tribes that most need that light—tribes in the United States of America. And within the United States, we have told some of these people groups that they are evil and should work harder to be more righteous in their own strength. We have claimed to love them from a distance, but we have failed to show them directly and personally that we are selfless, loving, and good. We vocally oppose them in mass media. We are absent in their personal lives, and then we claim with our words that we love them unconditionally.

Resurrecting God's mandate for good living among the pagans does not require a particular political position. But it requires that regardless of political conviction or doctrinal system, we re-elevate the goodness of our lives lived out *"among"* the pagans in our local communities—no matter what tribe those pagans belong to. That's what God repeatedly commands Christ's followers to do. That's His public relations plan.

Meeting the Lost Where They Are, It's What Christ Did

Remember Steph—the young woman who was enslaved in prostitution? God used an undeniably good evangelical to help draw Steph out of dark slavery. That goodness can't be claimed from a distance. It has to be demonstrated in person. Steph put it this way:

> How important it is to go into these dark places, because that's where the victims are comfortable. People are building pretty shelters and places that look really good, so the victims will come out of these dark places and come into this warm embrace. The idea is

amazing and noble, but the reality is that these victims want us to come to them in the jails and alleyways, in the pimp's apartments. When we come there and show them love, then that's when they're going to start being drawn out of those dark places. There's no way they're going to be drawn out of those dark places without going into those places ourselves.

Steph adds, "It's about meeting the victims where they're at, in the darkest places."

And isn't this exactly what Jesus did?

When God stepped down into darkness, He humbled himself to reach us. He didn't claim to love us from an impersonal distance. He proved it by meeting us in our world. He didn't tell us to get our acts together and then come to Him. He came to us. Now He calls us, as His representatives, to take His goodness into the dark places of society—to proactively demonstrate His nature and character.

Most evangelicals agree that to reach Steph and other minors enslaved in sex trafficking, we must employ a number of the same missionary assumptions we use to reach foreign tribes on other continents. We must suspend judgment, demonstrate unconditional acceptance, and anticipate that we'll be misunderstood. We must go into their place of darkness, while maintaining our personal integrity and purity. Even after conversion, we can expect someone from a foreign tribe and culture to take months or years to fully embrace new life in Christ. Their full freedom from slavery will be a long process.

We understand this with a teenage American girl who has been prostituted. But change that to a middle-aged man who is gay, and some evangelicals raise a double standard about how we treat those who don't know or fully understand Christ.

The following practical steps for showing God's goodness apply to every foreign tribe we find around us in our culture. Because evangelicalism is presently on a collision course with the tribe of the LGBT/homosexual movement and its many straight "allies" who share their offense against evangelicals, we will make that tribe a sort of case study, as we walk through these steps.

An Evangelical Invitation to the Homosexual Tribe

We often talk about an evangelical *response* to the homosexual movement. Based on the passages we've seen above—and on the model of Christ's incarnation—the idea of a *response* may be less biblical than the idea of a *proactive demonstration* of love and self-sacrifice.

Christ's incarnation was less a reaction or response than it was a proactive demonstration of love: "We love because he first loved us" (1 John 4:19).

God's love was not merely spoken or claimed from a distance or as a response. God proactively demonstrated His love in the very places where "sinners" hung out. He demonstrated His love to individuals—in tangible and undeniable ways—without compromising His own holiness. In the same way, to be like Christ, we must proactively demonstrate God's goodness and love to the individual homosexuals whom God places in each of our lives. When we make hollow claims of love from a distance, those claims do more harm than good.

Here are six practical steps for demonstrating God's goodness to the souls God loves in foreign United States tribes.

1. Take God's goodness directly to the homosexual tribe in your life and community. Don't wait for them to come to you.

God didn't wait for us to make our way to Him. He sought us, in the person of Jesus Christ (Luke 15). If we love any tribe in the vicinity where God plants us, we will go to them, as Christ came to us.

With the people group of homosexuals in the United States, we do well to first examine our own hearts for pride and sin, before reaching out. We should beware of our own tendency to react to, run from, or be hateful toward tribes that make us feel threatened or uncomfortable.

The reality is that you *will* directly bump into the homosexual tribe in your personal life—even if you live in an evangelical suburb on the buckle of the Bible Belt. Determine beforehand that when you encounter this tribe, you will not be shocked or defensive. You will not react. You will treat a soul from this tribe just as positively as a soul from any other tribe. Determine beforehand to thank God for an opportunity to directly show Christ and His goodness to another people group.

As you interact with folks from the homosexual tribe, acknowledge that many evangelicals have hated and wronged these tribes and their people. Just as Steph—the victim of teenage sexual trafficking—had been abused by so-called Christians, many from other tribes have been wronged by evangelicals. And so, as you show Christ's goodness to a homosexual, you may need to apologize for the behavior of other Christians.

We have, in many cases, treated the souls in our mission field as if they were the spiritual enemy—rather than hostages we are called to liberate from the enemy.

2. Refuse to classify the homosexual tribe as some worse class of sinners. This is unbiblical and showcases poor theology.

One of the most embarrassing gaffes of otherwise studied evangelicals today is this false hierarchy of sins. Due to a misunderstanding of Romans 1, some have said or implied things as ridiculous as "homosexuals are more sinful than other people."

Let's see what Jesus said. In His interactions we do not see a hierarchy of sins. Jesus spoke of people in only two groups: the lost and the found, the dark and the light, the sick and the healthy, and so forth. In these and so many other pairs, Jesus repeatedly clarifies that every person falls into one of just two categories: *separated* from God by sin, or *connected* to God by redemption.

It was the religious hypocrites—not Jesus—who created hierarchies of sins: tax collector, prostitute, and so forth. The Pharisees defined people by what they did. Jesus defined people by *Whom* they knew. God defines not by what people *do*, but by *Whom* they are related to: children of God or of Satan; friends of God or enemies of Him; and so forth.

In Jesus' view, all who are not yet reconciled to God fall into the same category—regardless of human labels. It was the Pharisees who categorized some sins as worse than others. Conveniently, this enabled them to place their own vices lowest on the list of offenses. And today, it is still the religious hypocrites among us who do the same. We act as if pride, jealousy, greed, and bitterness are less egregious sins—because they are *our* sins. The most egregious sins in our religious system are, conveniently, the ones that we are less attracted to ourselves.

In so doing we elevate our own earned righteousness, and we denigrate the unearned grace of God given to a population where "all have sinned." In God's view, *all* "fall short of the glory of God" (Romans 3:23). This equally includes the celibate, the moral priest, and the megachurch pastor, just as much as the people of the homosexual tribe.

Scripture never speaks of any one sin separating us from God *less* than other sins. All sin separates us from God. Incidentally, if we were to argue scripturally that any single sin is the "worst," that sin would not be homosexuality. It would be either religious hypocrisy or blasphemy against the Holy Spirit.

After all, Jesus was referring to a religious and moral people when He said, "If the miracles that were performed in you had been performed in Sodom, it would have remained to this day. But I tell you that it will be more bearable for Sodom on the day of judgment than for you" (Matthew 11:23–24). According to Jesus, who sees the hearts of men and women, these outwardly moral towns deserved more severe judgment than Sodom.

Furthermore, Ezekiel records this about Sodom's crime, in God's opinion: "This was the sin of your sister Sodom: She and her daughters were arrogant, overfed and unconcerned; they did not help the poor and needy" (Ezekiel 16:49).

Again, I don't believe God has a hierarchy of sins, especially not as it relates to salvation. We are either washed by the blood of the Lamb, or we are not. But the point is that, according to Ezekiel, being "arrogant, overfed and unconcerned" were the sins God most remembered about Sodom.

Frankly, I have some evangelical friends who are more "arrogant, overfed and unconcerned" than some of my homosexual unbelieving friends. And as for the sin of religious pride, few of my unbelieving friends from the homosexual tribe struggle with it, while plenty of my friends from the evangelical tribe do, including at times, myself.

The point is *not* to rank ourselves or others. The point is to remind us that scripturally and in spiritual reality, "all our righteous acts are like filthy rags" (Isaiah 64:6). That includes your self-righteous behavior and mine. None of us is justified because our particular vice is on the less-sinful list. We are only justified by the sacrifice of Christ at Calvary.

Therefore, we must determine beforehand that as we interact with the homosexual tribe in the United States, we will never treat any person as somehow worse than ourselves or others. If you're not sure how to do this, it may help to imagine that a person from the homosexual tribe is from the tribe of straight guys who view porn, or the tribe of straight women who gossip maliciously about other women. Each is equally separated from God apart from Christ, who loves them and gave himself for them. (And, like homosexuality, those behaviors are viewed as entirely acceptable in the host culture.)

No matter which tribe a soul hails from, if we expect an unbeliever to claim victory over sin in their own strength, then our expectations are out of line with Scripture. Such expectations dishonor Christ's blood shed at Calvary. To assume that nonbelievers can overcome sin—apart from Christ—is to imply that Christ is not *necessary* to overcome sin. And if that's the case, then the gospel is foolishness.

3. As with any tribe, don't focus on changing behavior. Focus on changing relationship to God through Christ.

To borrow from an old cliché, the horse must come before the cart. We evangelicals get this with alcoholism, pornography, heterosexual sex addiction, and so many other behaviors.

A person must come to Christ, and then *Christ* can free them from their slavery. But when it comes to homosexuality, many evangelicals swap the cart and the horse—expecting homosexual unbelievers to overcome their behavior without the power of the cross or the Holy Spirit.

Nowhere in the New Testament do we see God commanding a change of behavior apart from Christ, the Holy Spirit, or repentance. Even in the Old Testament, Jonah pleaded with Nineveh to repent—that is, to change their heart relationship to God—first. Only after repentance can behavior change permanently.

Prior to repentance and reconciliation through Jesus Christ, it is impossible for a nonbeliever to overcome sin—or to consistently change their behavior, in their own power. Is it any wonder that nonbelievers are exasperated by evangelicals constantly demanding they change something that they are, apart from Christ, unable to change?

When someone is addicted to alcohol, pornography, marijuana, or illicit heterosexual sex, we tell them (if we are scripturally sound) they need Christ's power to overcome that lifestyle. When someone from those same tribes comes to Christ, we expect them to be drawn to their former way of life. We expect that learning to walk with Christ will include some stumbles, falls, and retreats into those old entrenched patterns, as well documented by New Testament believers.

Again, we must double-check ourselves to make sure we are not raising a hypocritical double standard that classifies the struggle with the "old man" as okay for some but not for homosexuals or others.

No matter what tribe an unbeliever belongs to, we should lovingly expect them to act like pagans until they come to Christ.

4. Don't be surprised when you are hated and misunderstood about this issue. You will be.

As you interact with people from a foreign tribe, you will be misunderstood. No matter how high or pure your motives, you'll be mistaken for a bigot and a fraud. Jesus was.

Proactively love members of the homosexual tribe, and you will be misunderstood. Sometimes, we are misunderstood because we don't take the time to learn the tribe, their language, and values. Other times, we will never be properly understood—just as Christ and the apostles never were understood by many.

As the culture and its various tribes veer further away from anything remotely Christian, the chasm of assumptions, convictions, and deeply held values will grow wider and wider. As this chasm grows, you will be misunderstood. Some responses will be aggressive and unreasonably hateful. Don't be surprised.

Jesus cautioned, "If the world hates you, keep in mind that it hated me first. . . . If they persecuted me, they will persecute you also" (John 15:18, 20). The apostle Paul added, "Everyone who wants to live a godly life in Christ Jesus will be persecuted" (2 Timothy 3:12).

5. When you are hated or misunderstood, don't defend yourself or other evangelicals. Instead, let your quiet good actions eclipse any accusations.

Here's where we almost always go wrong. When we're misunderstood, attacked, or accused, we jump—often with good motives—to explain our motives or to defend the motives of other believers.

We don't see Christ or the apostles doing this very often. And they didn't need to, because their actions spoke louder than any words. If we will actively model God's goodness in personal and direct relationships, if we will apply God's unconditional love to every tribe in our own sphere, then we won't need to defend ourselves with words, even when we're misunderstood.

We also should refuse to defend ourselves verbally for a practical reason: It backfires, nearly every time. On national stages and in private conversations, when evangelicals attempt to defend their position on homosexuality, they almost always dig themselves deeper and deeper. The emotions get heated on both sides, and the blunders multiply.

Successful 21st-Century Evangelicals will put less stock in words and more stock in actions—proving that we are undeniably good to the individual homosexuals around us, no matter what anyone might say about us. When you find yourself tempted to speak up and defend yourself or others, transfer all that energy into undeniably good actions toward the homosexuals who are closest to you in your circles of relationship. As Peter and Paul both write time and again, we live in a hostile culture quietly with gentleness and respect and undeniable goodness—not drawing attention to ourselves, but serving selflessly, as Christ served.

Everywhere the apostles went, we see them doing the good deeds of healing, feeding widows, casting out demons, providing for the poor, and preaching the gospel of Christ. Despite these good deeds, they were routinely attacked, beaten, threatened, and in some cases murdered. Consistently, they did not defend themselves. They fearlessly proclaimed the Good News, while doing good deeds, all the while entrusting their safety and their reputation into God's hands (see Acts 18–20 in particular).

Loving "sinners" from some tribes in the United States will attract hate and accusations—not only from those tribes but also from the religiously proud. Jesus' life demonstrates this. He was rejected and abused—not only by the "sinners" He came to rescue, but also by the religious hypocrites who slandered Him for His extravagant love toward those sinners.

Jesus didn't defend himself to the accusers on either side. Rather, He lived out love in undeniable, self-sacrificial actions. His humility showed in His lack of concern to justify or explain himself to critics. He was, after all, not after their approval, but after the Father's. And the Father had sent Him specifically to seek out the lost and show love to sinners (Luke 15; Mark 2:13–17; John 3:17). Jesus knew His motives. The more our motives align with His, the less we'll feel the pull to defend ourselves with words.

Charles Spurgeon put it well when he described Jesus' controlled silence during His crucifixion trial: "The anvil breaks a host of hammers by quietly bearing their blows."[6]

In the culture conflicts exploding around us we have an opportunity to be like Christ—the Suffering Servant—in remarkable ways.

6. Keep on demonstrating God's goodness and unconditional love—to the homosexuals closest to you.

New Testament churches seem most concerned with the individual souls whom God, in His providence, placed in their proximity.

It's helpful for us to acknowledge that people function in tribes. As we do, we also have to acknowledge that every individual has their own unique belief system, wounds, and concerns—especially in the 21st century.

Few of us will be called as missionaries to the nationwide United States tribe of homosexuals. But every single one of us is already called as a missionary to the individual homosexuals God has placed in our own sphere of relationships.

Have you gone out of your way to ever show God's goodness in actions to the homosexuals in your neighborhood, social network, workplace, or family?

No matter how you are misunderstood or attacked by any tribe, simply continue living as Christ lived—taking God's goodness directly to the people He places closest to you. When you need encouragement, read the book of 2 Peter. Perhaps more than any other New Testament book, it helps us embrace our true position in the culture—by God's definitions.

In the end, we live daily with the hope that God will use our goodness "among the pagans" to glorify His name. We can live with the certainty that we will indeed find rest from hate and attack—in eternity with Christ. We need not seek our own personal comfort or justice in this world. Christ is preparing those for us.

And so, we personally and practically demonstrate God's goodness in undeniable and tangible ways to the people God places in our own lives—no matter which tribe they identify with.

Writer Margaret Feinberg casts a tangible vision of what this goodness could look like in our lifetimes:

> I would hope people would look at us and say, "Those Christians are the ones who run in when everyone else is running out. Those Christians are the ones who didn't give up on the crumbling inner cities. Those Christians are the ones who brought peace to Darfur. Those Christians are the ones who put an end to human trafficking. Those Christians are the ones who helped win the war on AIDS around the world. Those Christians are the ones who write those incredible lyrics, pen those unforgettable books, and create artwork that's mesmerizing. Those Christians are the ones who helped my mother when she got Alzheimer's. Those Christians are the ones who were kind to me when I was new to the area. Those Christians are the ones that made me want to believe in God."[7]

Jim Elliot went to a hostile tribe in 1956, and his blood ran into a river in Ecuador.

Jesus Christ went into a hostile world, and His blood ran from the foot of the cross.

As we go to hostile tribes in a hostile world, we will bleed, too. We *will* be attacked.

We must stop acting so surprised that a pagan society, with its many tribes, would be hostile toward us. It's time we stopped firing arrows at the hostages we're called to rescue. It's time we start going into the darkness with undeniable goodness. It's time we sacrifice ourselves as Christ did: "God made him who had no sin to be sin for us" (2 Corinthians 5:21).

We have noted that each of the church's present declines tests our loyalty: Are we more committed to American evangelical culture, or to Christ and His radical message? No issue today tests that loyalty more than our response to the hateful culture around us. Will we behave as Christ and His apostles? Or will we react defensively, as many American evangelicals have during the late 20th century? Will we press in to become like Christ and Paul in proactively showing God's goodness to a hostile and hateful culture? Or will we do the human thing and respond as our forefathers taught us?

In Romans 9:2–3, Paul explains his passionate love for the Israeli people of his time. He says that, if it were possible, he would trade his own salvation so that they might be saved. Listen to the emotion in his words: "I have great sorrow and unceasing anguish in my heart. For I could wish that I myself were cursed and cut off from Christ for the sake of my brothers."

Now, consider that the ones Paul would trade his salvation for were the very ones who beat, stoned, dragged, stripped, flogged, scourged, imprisoned, berated, and left him for dead (2 Corinthians 11:25; Acts 16:22 and 14:19).

The hostilities we encounter today—and in the coming decades—may seem severe to us. They are often soft next to the hostilities encountered by Christ, by Stephen, by Paul, and by so many of Christ's people through the centuries.

Will we respond with self-sacrificing genuine love and concern, as Christ and His apostles did?

Or will we respond in self-defense, fear, and reaction, as human nature does?

9

Uniting

How to Unite a Divided Church

Make every effort to keep the unity of the Spirit through the bond of peace. There is one body and one Spirit—just as you were called to one hope when you were called . . . one God and Father of all, who is over all and through all and in all.

Ephesians 4:3–6

I never got to attend a Billy Graham crusade. But on August 28, 2011, I got a small taste. That night a massive crowd of evangelical believers gathered at the city courthouse in Prescott, Arizona, to worship Christ. It was a big gathering for a little city. We had thousands of men and women from dozens of churches.

Worship leaders and pastors from six evangelical churches shared a stage—leading and pointing the body of Christ to the Head of the body. We worshiped in unity—lifting the name and message of Jesus Christ. We ended up calling it the Night of Worship, and it's becoming a tradition in our neck of the woods. Believers from dozens of churches have told us how long they have prayed and hoped for a gathering of local churches.

How did God make it happen? As He almost always does, He used an available leader. A gifted worship pastor from a large church chose to use all his influence, clout, and event budget—not to draw attention to himself or his church, but to Jesus Christ.

In the end, no single congregation's name was on the event. No worship leader or teacher was named or known. But Christ was named and known by thousands. It was a powerful scene not only for us small-town evangelicals—but also for the nonbelieving community we serve.

Jesus prayed this for His church in the United States and elsewhere: "May they be brought to complete unity . . ." (John 17:23). Why did He pray this? Well, in His own words, ". . . to let the world know that you sent me."

Did you catch that? According to Jesus, the world will know the Father sent Him *because* of our unity with His other followers. Here Jesus is praying not just for His twelve disciples but for "those who will believe in me through their message" (v. 20).

As more United States evangelicals divide over politics and other issues, how can we nationally become an answer to Jesus' prayer for "complete unity"? And, in an age of pluralism, subjective truth, and false teachers, how do we unify around Christ's truth without compromising that truth in the process?

These are not easy times to unify biblically. Next to Jesus' own words, perhaps the most practical quote about evangelical unity is this truism: "In essentials, unity. In non-essentials, charity. In all things, Christ." This axiom identifies the spine that held 20th-century evangelicalism together, and it gives us an outline for biblical unity as 21st-Century Evangelicals.

Our unity must give and insist on clear boundaries about the essentials.

Our unity must grant gracious room to disagree on non-essentials.

And our unity must exalt Christ and His gospel.

The Simple Formula for Evangelical Unity

Why does unity matter? We started this journey by examining the downsized reality that evangelicals only account for about

7 percent of the United States population. In sheer count, that's still a remarkable number—about 22 million people. Can you imagine the power and influence of 22 million united, committed, and organized people?

My favorite picture of unity is a YouTube video titled "Battle at Kruger." It was filmed on a South African safari and has since been viewed some 65 million times. If you haven't seen it, you should check it out now.

In the clip, four lions pounce on three Cape buffalo as the buffalo drink from a watering hole. The Cape buffalo—mother, father, and calf—scatter when attacked. The four lions get hold of the tiny calf, and it doesn't look good. Gnawing, biting, tearing, and dragging, the lions fight to bring the calf to the ground. It's buffalo versus lion. Then, some crocodiles also get in on what seems to be a food fight. The little buffalo has no way of retaliating. All he can do is hang in there. Somehow he stays up on all four hooves.

That's when the herd shows up. At least a hundred Cape buffalo. A solid wall of muscle and horns encircles the four lions. The largest, strongest bulls stand side by side, forming a battering ram of horns at the front of the mass. One at a time, the largest bulls take turns charging the lions.

One bull gores a lion, throwing it ten feet in the air. The other lions keep gnawing at the calf, which is still alive, but now out of the water and away from the crocodiles. The lions don't take the herd seriously—until another lion gets gored. And another gets stampeded.

Finally, the calf breaks free from the last lion, and the largest bulls chase the pride of lions away. What no single buffalo could do alone—attack, frighten, and chase away four lions—the community of buffalo could easily do together. In the end, the calf walked away without a limp.

One animal expert explained that Cape buffalo typically function in various individual groups and even fight with each other (sounds like some of our dear evangelical churches and ministries, right?). But, she added, "If a youngster is threatened, both the harem males and bachelor males—which usually fight with one another—will get together to try to rescue it."[1]

We have seen that combative spiritual forces are tearing apart the United States evangelical church. Like the Cape buffalo, we need powerful evangelicals who "usually fight with one another" to "get together to try to rescue" the movement. We need the humility and perspective to see that our movement is under spiritual attack, and we need each other. I'm not arguing for community worship gatherings or any one specific model. I'm arguing—from Scripture—for the biblical value of unity. If we adopt this value in our own cities and corners of the kingdom, we can link shoulders in creative ways to defend our children and to advance Christ's love and hope in the United States.

Three Cape buffalo didn't stand a chance against four lions, but hundreds of buffalo easily prevailed. Some herds of Cape buffalo in Tanzania number into the thousands. Viewed from a helicopter, they bind together into a massive moving river of black and brown muscle, cutting across the African plains. Imagine the spiritual view of 22 million evangelicals, moving in unity, following Christ's commands for His church.

Unity is power and is important for practical reasons. But our highest motivation for unity is that God commands it. Christ desires it so severely that He prayed it for us during His earthly ministry. The Holy Spirit also inspired the apostles to command and explain evangelical unity in passages like Ephesians 4, Romans 15, and others.

> Make *every effort* to keep the unity of the Spirit through the bond of peace.
> There is one body and one Spirit—just as you were called to one hope when you were called . . . one God and Father of all, who is over all and through all and in all.
>
> Ephesians 4:3–6

> May the God who gives endurance and encouragement give you a spirit of unity among yourselves as you follow Christ Jesus, so that with one heart and mouth you may glorify the God and Father of our Lord Jesus Christ. Accept one another, then, just as Christ accepted you, in order to bring praise to God.
>
> Romans 15:5–7

A Call to 21st-Century Evangelicalism, Intentionally Led by Biblical Leaders

Unity doesn't happen by accident. Even Cape buffalo need leaders—strong, proven, courageous leaders who will stick their necks out to chase predators away. With His people, God has always chosen to use human leaders, even though He doesn't need them. From Moses and David to Peter and Paul, God chooses and uses human leaders to unify and direct His people in His plans.

I am calling evangelical leaders, and young leaders especially, to join in solidifying a unified national evangelical movement. I'm calling us to be 21st-Century Evangelicals—by uniting around an ageless, changeless Savior and message. I'm calling next-generation leaders, at national and local levels, to band together in saying that we have great charity and liberty in non-essentials, but we also have great clarity and rigor in the essentials. Let's examine the essential boundaries within which we unify.

"In Essentials, Unity"

Just as we must protect from divisiveness within, we must also guard against boundary deconstruction on the perimeters. The National Association of Evangelicals' Statement of Faith, the Apostles Creed, the Westminster Confession, and other common creeds outline the widely accepted evangelical essentials. These core essentials include

- the Trinity
- the depravity of man
- substitutionary atonement
- Christ's complete humanity and complete deity
- the sufficiency and exclusivity of Christ's work
- the need for a personal relationship with Christ

In recent years, some of these core tenets have been disputed in mainstream evangelical circles. But if we continue allowing evangelical essentials to be blurred and redefined, we will continue to see our movement disintegrate and dissolve. Without clear boundaries, we have no true power or unity. Without clear boundaries, we have no movement. After all, even Cape buffalo know the difference between another buffalo, a lion, and a crocodile. Even wild beasts know their own kind.

In an age of pluralism and postmodern approaches to truth, we need clarity and boldness about the evangelical essentials. We need to be able to spot an evangelical. And we need to be able to spot someone who means well, who may even be a broadly historical Christian, but who is not an evangelical.

Jesus and the apostles repeatedly warned that false teachers would come from within the church, as wolves attacking the flock. It is the duty of biblical leaders to "be on your guard" for false teachers (Acts 20:28–31).

Of all these important essentials, none is more practically important today than *the essential doctrine of the authority of Scripture.*

The first lines of the nursery song "Jesus Loves Me" capture two of the most basic evangelical essentials: "Jesus loves me this I know" and "for the Bible tells me so."

In this didactic tune, we remind our youngsters that the reason we know Jesus loves us is *because* His Word tells us so. Recently, some who claim to be evangelical are suggesting we can emphasize Jesus' love, while doubting the accuracy or authority of Jesus' Word.

Such a claim contradicts the most basic truths of evangelical Christianity. For hundreds of years, we evangelicals have arrived at every one of our essential doctrines for one simple reason: They are our best understanding of what the Bible instructs. Quite simply, without the authority of Scripture we would not have our history, our foundation, our movement, or our theology.

We evangelicals believe Scripture is authoritative, true, understandable, and infallible. This is an essential. And it's one that we must fearlessly fortify, in order to protect the coherence, unity, and purpose of the movement.

Quietly, our foundational belief in Scripture has been eroding along various edges of the movement. In some "evangelical" circles, the authority of Scripture has been overlooked in the noise and flash of modern progress. Other teachers are painting over scriptural authority, accepting Scripture as a narrative but not as objective truth.

Mark Galli of *Christianity Today* observed this deterioration when he wrote, "To be an evangelical used to mean one stood for certain theological convictions—penal substitution, inerrancy, and so forth—but now many evangelicals take delight in defining themselves over and against one of these formerly cardinal doctrines, while insisting on the right to be called evangelicals."[2]

I believe it's time we graciously call such revisions what they are: non-evangelical. While we love those who disagree with our high view of Scripture, we can also be clear that teachers who do not hold to Scripture's authority are not historically or theologically evangelical.

- We believe 2 Timothy 3:16–17 when it says, "*All* Scripture is God-breathed and is useful for teaching, rebuking, correcting and training in righteousness, so that the man of God may be thoroughly equipped for every good work."
- We believe Proverbs 30:5: "*Every* word of God is flawless."
- We believe Romans 15:4: "*Everything* that was written in the past was written to teach us, so that through the endurance taught in the Scriptures and the encouragement they provide we might have hope."

I'm calling evangelical leaders across the United States to put a flag in the ground, to graciously proclaim in unity that the movement away from scriptural authority is not the direction of 21st-Century Evangelicalism. In fact, when a teacher or writer chooses to deconstruct scriptural authority, he or she chooses to walk out the clearly marked exit of our movement.

The essentialness of scriptural authority is well illustrated in this extended quote from Francis Schaeffer's *The Great Evangelical Disaster*:

Not far from where we live in Switzerland is a high ridge of rock with a valley on both sides. One time I was there when there was snow on the ground along that ridge. The snow was lying there unbroken, a seeming unity. However, that unity was an illusion, for it lay along a great divide; it lay along a watershed. One portion of the snow when it melted would flow into one valley. The snow which lay close beside would flow into another valley when it melted.

Now it just so happens on that particular ridge that the melting snow which flows down one side of that ridge goes down into a valley, into a small river, and then down into the Rhine River. The Rhine then flows on through Germany and the water ends up in the cold waters of the North Sea. The water from the snow that started out so close along that watershed on the other side of the ridge, when this snow melts, drops off sharply down the ridge into the Rhone Valley. This water flows into Lac Leman—or as it is known in the English-speaking world, Lake Geneva—and then goes down below that into the Rhone River which flows through France and into the warm waters of the Mediterranean.

The snow lies along that watershed, unbroken, as a seeming unity. But when it melts, where it ends in its destinations is literally a thousand miles apart. That is a watershed. That is what a watershed is. A watershed divides. A clear line can be drawn between what seems at first to be the same or at least very close, but in reality ends in very different situations. In a watershed there is a line. . . .

Evangelicals today are facing a watershed concerning the nature of biblical inspiration and authority. It is a watershed issue in very much the same sense as described in the illustration. Within evangelicalism there are a growing number who are modifying their views on the inerrancy of the Bible so that the full authority of Scripture is completely undercut. But it is happening in very subtle ways. Like the snow lying side-by-side on the ridge, the new views on biblical authority often seem at first glance not to be so very far from what evangelicals, until just recently, have always believed. But also, like the snow lying side-by-side on the ridge, the new views when followed consistently end up a thousand miles apart.[3]

✦ We can be close-minded, narrow, and obstinate about the doctrine of Scripture—because history has demonstrated the alternative. The decline of many mainline denominations in the 1900s demonstrates that no matter how high the motives, to welcome lower views of Scripture leads, every time, to the demise of the church within a couple of generations. This is documented history, and yet some of the most exciting new "evangelical" leaders are now tearing down the authority of Scripture, as if we hadn't seen its destructive end, just within the last century.

- The Scriptures were Jesus' rule (Matthew 22:29 and Luke 4:4, 8, 12).
- The Scriptures were the apostles' authority (Acts 17:2; 18:28; and Romans 4:3; 16:26).
- The Scriptures were the New Testament church's guidebook (Acts 17:11 and Romans 1:2).
- The Scriptures must remain our objectively true standard for faith and practice (2 Timothy 3:16).
- Without the Scriptures, we do not have the gospel or Jesus (1 Corinthians 15:3 and Galatians 3:22).
- To lose the Scriptures is to lose Jesus and His message. The two are inextricably linked—as attested by their mutual testimony.

Instead of giving attention, stages, headlines, and prominence to post-biblical teachers who claim to be evangelical, we should be clarifying the boundaries and then ignoring those outside the boundary of scriptural infallibility. Paul wrote this of self-proclaimed prophets in his time: "If anybody thinks he is a prophet or spiritually gifted, let him acknowledge that what I am writing to you is the Lord's command. If he ignores this [the Lord's command], he himself will be ignored" (1 Corinthians 14:37–38).

We have not ignored those who ignore "the Lord's command[s]." We have fed into their thirst for controversy and given them great publicity. As a result, we have propelled their influence, their fame, and their rich profits.

God is the judge of souls, motives, and destinies (Romans 14:10–12), but we can rightly judge if individuals and ministries are honoring God's Word (Acts 17:11). Indeed, it is "noble" for us to do this with "eagerness." The Bereans judged whether Paul's teaching was truth or error by measuring his words against the objective standard of Scripture. We can and must do the same today.

Dr. R. Albert Mohler Jr. summarizes the erosion of this foundational doctrine. He explains our evangelical forbearers' struggle to protect the authority of Scripture in their time. They blazed a difficult trail away from theological liberals, even as they resisted the petty hyperseparatism of fundamentalism:

> But the founders of the evangelical movement . . . saw themselves as protecting this doctrinal inheritance from marginalization on the right and from accommodation on the left. They feared that fundamentalism was fighting over many of the wrong issues even as the liberals were tearing down the house.[4]

And lest we forget, Mohler reminds us of the blood and sweat that have been invested into protecting our movement's freedom within boundaries.

> [Early evangelicals] left positions, pulpits, and pensions [in liberal denominations] behind as they did what they believed fidelity to Christ and the substance of biblical Christianity required. Now, all that the early evangelicals sought to defend is under sustained subversion from within the movement they gave their lives to build.[5]

It's our time to defend the essentials of evangelicalism, even as we enjoy the liberties of it. Successful evangelicals, while modeling love and grace within the boundaries, will be rigorous in rebuilding and fortifying the infallibility of Scripture and the other non-negotiable boundaries of our movement.

"In Non-Essentials, Charity"

The entire law is summed up in a single command: "Love your neighbor as yourself." If you keep on biting and devouring each other, watch out or you will be destroyed by each other.

Galatians 5:14–15

Graciously disagreeing within clear boundaries is the DNA of the unique evangelicalism we have inherited from Billy Graham, Carl F. H. Henry, Harold Ockenga, and so many others. In the

20th century, separatist fundamentalism, with its divisive internal boundaries, ate and devoured itself to the point of starvation. Soft liberalism, with its lack of external boundaries, diluted itself to the point of being unrecognizable as Christian.

It was the balance of tenacious outer boundaries and gracious inner disagreements that made United States evangelicalism so globally powerful and unique. We evangelicals have a rich heritage of balance within truth—a heritage worth protecting, not only because the 20th century proved its power, but also because Scripture demands such a marriage of grace and truth, unity, and clarity.

Just as some evangelicals are drifting toward liberalism, others are now reacting to the extreme of a new fundamentalism. With good intent, they are sacrificing grace on the altar of truth. True evangelicalism is uncompromising on the essentials and unconditionally gracious on the non-essentials.

God's Word records the early church learning to graciously disagree on non-essential beliefs and practices. These non-essentials are important matters, but not so important as to divide the body of Christ. In the context of internal disputes, God instructs the following through Paul: "One man considers one day more sacred than another; another man considers every day alike. Each one should be fully convinced in his own mind" (Romans 14:5).

The greatest strength of evangelicalism in the 20th century was its ability to apply Romans 14:5 to so many non-essentials, even while holding to the essentials. Safe within the protection of the essentials, we can increasingly agree to disagree on peripheral matters.

We can substitute so many modern controversies into Romans 14:5, and the timeless principle applies.

One considers Calvinism more sacred than Arminianism.

One considers contemporary more sacred than traditional.

One considers sign-gifts more sacred than the other.

One considers believer's baptism more sacred than infant baptism.

One considers free grace more sacred than lordship.

One considers Republican more sacred than Democrat.

One considers the Tea Party more sacred than either.

One considers dispensational more sacred than covenant.

One considers eternal security more than "by their fruit you will know them."

In each of these, and so many other internal disputes, we can apply the latter half of Romans 14:5: "Each one should be fully convinced in his own mind."

To grasp the text in today's context, we might fill today's non-essential controversies into the blanks of Romans 14:6–8: "He who regards _____(Republican)_____ as special, does so to the Lord. He who _____(votes Democrat)_____, _____(votes)_____ to the Lord, for he gives thanks to God; and he who _____(worships with or without sign-gifts)_____, does so to the Lord and gives thanks to God. For none of us lives to himself alone and none of us dies to himself alone. If we live, we live to the Lord; and if we die, we die to the Lord. So, whether we live or die, we belong to the Lord."

In this journey we have learned much about our true standing in the culture. What does it all mean? In part, it means we no longer have the luxury of dividing ourselves internally. We no longer have the size, the strength, the momentum, or the footing in the culture to waste energy fighting against each other over non-essentials.

Remember the Cape buffalo, who, as one animal expert said, "typically fight with each other." What if the strong males had not unified to protect the calf at the "Battle of Kruger"? The lions wouldn't have just eaten one calf. They would have had a feast, along with the crocodiles.

Our enemy, whom God describes as a prowling and roaring lion, is presently bloody around the mouth, enjoying such a feast on our young people. The flock that God entrusted to our oversight is scattered, divided, bleeding, and declining. Will we continue infighting over non-essentials? Or will we unite to protect our young?

Unifying Politically Divided Evangelicals

Of all the disputes and divisions in the church today, none is as heated, as passionate, and as splitting as our disagreement over United States politics. How do we unite evangelicals who disagree within our own ministries, churches, or families? I'd like to offer a few practical principles to unify your ministry, church, or family during the next decades.

First, in light of all we've seen above, we must acknowledge that political views are important, and they will always be a matter of passion. But they are not theological essentials. American evangelicals have disagreed on politics since the birth of the United States. During the Revolutionary War, many Bible-believing Christians were pacifists, even as many other Bible-believing Christians were patriots. We will gather at the throne with both groups in heaven.

Forward-thinking evangelicals will respect the political diversity within the body of Christ today. They will intentionally avoid associating Christ's message with any one political party or politician. Such positioning will ensure that these ministries do not become victims of the political rifts now rupturing in churches and denominations.

Ministries that decide to overtly associate with the religious right or the evangelical political left should do so with an awareness that those associations will alienate their ministry from many devoted believers. Keep in mind that it's now a near 40/60 split between right and non-right evangelicals. Strong associations or endorsements to either side will, as a result, isolate roughly one half of the body of Christ. Hyperpatriotic or anti-patriotic messages will both have the effect of dividing the people in your ministry.

I believe this respectful "room to disagree" position can be held in a way that encourages and applauds a person's political activism as an honorable expression of their own convictions.

Ministries that truly seek to elevate the gospel and unify the church around Christ will avoid heavy political associations, even as they encourage individual liberty for those who are particularly patriotic or politically involved.

What to Expect Politically in the 21st-Century Evangelical Church

If you haven't already met them within reach of your ministry, expect to meet the following diverse groups in coming years:

- Young seminary graduates who are theologically conservative and who also believe in global warming, nuclear disarmament, international debt forgiveness, and that Palestine should be a state, with land.
- Young professional and educated evangelicals who are passionate about Jesus, about social justice, and about Democrat politics, too.
- Middle-aged evangelicals who are leery about any marrying of Jesus and political involvement.
- Baby boomer and older evangelicals who are active members of the Tea Party—and who may want to promote the Tea Party or Republican candidates during a Sunday worship service.
- Midwestern or southern evangelicals who are true believers and also truly believe the Republican Party is synonymous with evangelicalism.

When folks ask your ministry to endorse a specific political candidate or position, you might let them know that their position is respected, but that there is room in your ministry to respectfully disagree on earthly politics. If a person sees political positions as essential, they may be more comfortable in a ministry that actively takes a more separatist position on these important but non-essential matters. There will always be some evangelicals in these fringes on both the right and left.

The position I am advocating here is not new. It is exactly how Billy Graham operated. As he modeled, I would remind us that to make any earthly political position a litmus of orthodoxy is not scripturally, historically, or philosophically evangelical. To withdraw from or criticize other believers because of their earthly political positions is philosophically separatist and divisive. It elevates a non-biblical matter to a level of biblical importance.

While boldly guarding the outer perimeters of evangelicalism, we must begin obeying God's Word when it says to "make every effort to keep the unity of the Spirit" within (Ephesians 4:3). Whether we like each other or not, we need each other. And we are commanded to love each other.

This applies to our political infighting. Democrat or Republican, liberal or conservative, Socialist or capitalist—important as these camps are, they are not evangelical essentials. They are mortal issues and are not worthy of dividing the immortal body of Christ.

In the coming years and decades we will see more churches and ministries take positions that mimic the fundamentalist versus liberal extremes of the 1900s. Some will react and retreat into defensive separatism, even as others capitulate to the culture and drift into defenseless pluralism. These extremes are the natural reactions to abrupt changes in the culture and church.

To foster biblical unity, we must be intentional and discerning so that we avoid both these extremes as we guide Christ's bride through these difficult decades. Both the hyper-separatism of fundamentalism and the open boundaries of theological liberalism proved to destroy churches and denominations during the last eighty years. Let's pray for humble confidence and godly grace to not repeat these mistakes with the souls we shepherd.

If evangelicalism has any hope of regrouping and becoming a nimbler, more focused, and spiritually capable movement, we must learn again to unify, despite differences, within the essentials. Our local neighborhoods and ministry communities are the best place for us to begin applying this. Have you met the other evangelical leaders in your city—even those who disagree on non-essentials? Do you pray for them or with them?

United States evangelicals tasted the power of unification at the height of the Billy Graham era. Will we protect and nourish the rich heritage handed down to us? Or will we neglect it—either by fighting within or by passively allowing non-evangelical personalities to deconstruct the outer walls?

10

Solvent

How to Recession-Proof Your Ministry, Financially

"Where your treasure is, there your heart will be also."

Jesus, in Luke 12:34

I am not a prosperity or health-and-wealth preacher. I do not wear a watch, let alone an expensive one. I buy most of my clothes secondhand. I am a pastor.

So it's only natural that people have questions when I pull up to the church building in, say, a brand-new Jaguar XKR convertible, which looks a lot like a $200,000 Aston Martin. First, I explain that it isn't an Aston Martin. It's only a Jaguar. The sticker price is "only" $117,000. Then, I explain why I am seen driving a different new car each week.

When I was an editor at *The Scottsdale Times*, I created a syndicated auto column. Auto manufacturers—Toyota, GM, Mercedes, and so forth—deliver brand-new vehicles to my home. I drive each vehicle for a week, and then I write a review for each car, truck, or SUV. The column prints in a handful of magazines across the country. I've continued writing the column as a pastor. (And yes, it's a tough job, but somebody has to do it.)

Why do I say all this? Because I love the internal combustion engine as much as anyone. One of my first cars was a gas-guzzling V-8 Mustang. Today's little hybrids are okay. Itsy-bitsy four-cylinder gas misers are practical, sure. But if you want to hear me giggle aloud like a little girl, put me in the seat of a 650-horsepower Shelby GT500. Watch as I fishtail the car, sprint to 100 mph, stomp the brakes, then do it again. Over and over.

In my perfect motoring existence, I would roar through empty country roads, windows down, propelled by a gas-devouring V-8. But here's the sad reality. No matter how much I love gasoline engines, the day will likely come when the earth runs out of affordable crude oil. It could be fifty years from now, or it could be three hundred years.

A day will come when gas stations are bulldozed. And on that day, a Jaguar convertible, a Hummer, even a Lamborghini will be of little practical value. What good is a powerful gasoline vehicle, if the world has no fuel?

The fossil fuel crisis may be centuries away. But the evangelical fuel crisis—the crisis of donations—is already upon us. In chapter 4 we saw the trending decrease in evangelical donations. Unless generational patterns change radically, many ministries will see revenue decrease by 50 to 70 percent in the next ten to thirty years.

And so the question, What good will a dynamic 20th-century ministry model be if that ministry has no fuel? What good is a national teaching ministry, a megachurch, a missions agency, or a Christian college if that ministry does not have enough fuel to operate?

Without a rapid flow of cash, our sharpest, shiniest ministries will be Lamborghinis with empty gas tanks. Pretty, but impractical. And ultimately, relics.

Donations across the United States have already begun drying up. It is the beginning of a drought that will worsen for three decades. If these trends do not change, surviving ministries may eventually be functioning on 30 percent of their 2013 budgets.

The shortage will not happen overnight. We have a closing window during which to prepare. Ministry leaders can begin building "alternative" vehicles now. These vehicles may not be as much fun to drive. But the point is that they still *will drive* in fifteen to thirty years—when ministry Hummers and gas-guzzlers are left for dead in the desert.

These new ministry vehicles need not run *without* the fuel of donations. They just need to run on *less* fuel. *Ultimately, they will depend less on dollars and more on disciples.*

Burdened with budget concerns and day-to-day minutia, few ministries have the macro-vision to create donation-sipping vehicles. When giving decreases, we limp along. Like drivers of large SUVs paying four dollars per gallon for gasoline, we might inflate our tires and clean our air filter to slightly improve gas mileage. But we haven't considered trading in the Hummer for a gas sipper. We haven't considered changing our entire model.

Until now, good ministries have not needed to run on less fuel. For American evangelicals, the 20th century was a lot like the 1990s, when gas cost less than one dollar per gallon. Why pinch out miles per gallon when a gallon of gas costs less than a candy bar?

After such a century, ministries have become addicted to donations. So much so that when giving drops, we only know to cut staff or facilities. In either case, the net "ministry" decreases. Many of us literally do not know how to do ministry without hundreds of thousands or millions of dollars.

Have we considered that our model may be outdated? Could we be doing *more* with *less*? On the surface, this might seem impossible. But in the models and mandates of the New Testament, we find four practical ways to do more ministry with less money.

1. *Hybrid Ministry*: Learn and launch ministry models that do not depend solely on paid staff.
2. *Conservation*: Avoid debt obligations beyond the next ten years.
3. *Preparation*: Teach mature givers about the evangelical recession and create legacy vehicles, such as bequeathals or ministry trusts, so their gifts can outlive them.
4. *Abandon*: Disciple the church in life surrender and biblical giving.

1. Hybrid Ministry: Learn and launch ministry models that do not depend solely on paid staff.

Doing more with less is easy to talk about—and difficult to do. I remember when the first Toyota Prius and other early hybrid cars hit the streets. A hybrid, as you may know, generates electricity when the car stops or coasts. It then uses both an electric and a gasoline engine—so that the gasoline engine works less and uses less fuel.

When hybrids first arrived, they were real nuisances. Some were slower than golf carts. On one model, the air conditioner would turn off at stoplights—something Arizona auto critics noted during 115-degree summers.

But in the last ten years, automakers have radically improved hybrids. These once impractical toys have matured into practical cars and SUVs. Some hybrids now drive as comfortably as "normal" gasoline cars, while delivering fifty miles per gallon in the city. It has taken a decade of intentional work, but hybrids are now doing far more with much less.

The best hybrids rule the pack because their makers have been working on them the longest. Toyota and Honda started working on a solution before other automakers believed there was even a problem. Now they are thriving in a 21st-century market, where many buyers value gas mileage.

In the same way, ministries that begin working on hybrid ministry models *now* will be ahead of the curve when the fuel crisis leaves other ministries stalled on the sidelines or sitting in the fuel line, begging fewer donors for more dollars.

What do I mean by a hybrid ministry model? One that still runs on donations—but requires less money to produce more ministry. Hybrid ministries don't require as much money because they've been careful about output (building and other overhead costs), and they also have an alternate energy source (nonpaid staff).

Hybrid autos use an alternate energy source—electricity—to reduce the need for fuel. In ministry, the alternate energy source is disciples, or unpaid staff. Unpaid or alternative staff can greatly reduce the need for donation fuel, while also moving us toward a more biblical gift-based and disciple-based model.

By unpaid and alternative staff, I do not mean volunteers who require constant monitoring and prodding from paid staff. I mean trained, called, qualified, and gifted staff and pastors, who work tent-making jobs and do not draw full-time salaries from the church. Realistically, these nonpaid staff will not be putting in as many hours as paid staff, but there is no limit to the number of nonpaid staff a ministry can add to the team.

Ironically, the hybrid ministry model forces us back to discipleship in the local church. *Leaders who imitate Christ's small-team discipleship model can "engineer" and "build" auxiliary engines in the next ten years.* This is already being done with great success in some churches. Unfortunately, they are the exceptions.

Laura Ortberg Turner wrote this about the less-than-biblical divide we typically see between staff and laypeople:

> We have on our hands a Christian celebrity culture that runs counter to the gospel: that elevates the gifted communicators, teachers, and leaders and devalues the gifts of the volunteers: those who welcome people into their homes, the administrative assistants, and the janitors. . . . It is sad, and it is wrong, and it is against everything that Jesus tells us and lived out about the crux of his gospel being located in service.[1]

As we train new leaders, God will call some into traditional "full-time" ministry. But—aware of the pending fuel crisis in evangelicalism—we can teach many new leaders their value in the secular marketplace, as leaders who do not draw full-time wages from the congregation. This is, after all, how the apostle Paul served the New Testament churches Christ called him to plant and feed.

A Case Study in Hybrid Ministry

Let's say that a church of 600 has five full-time staff pastors today. If that church does not plan for the 50-percent decrease in giving over the next fifteen years, it will be forced to cut its paid staff, probably in half. As a result, it will lose half of its pastoral "ministry."

But let's say that right now the same church hires or reassigns a pastor for focused training of lay staff members. In the next fifteen years this pastor trains up ten part-time and alternative pastors. These pastors or staff members meet biblical qualifications for leadership. They are publicly commissioned, but they are not paid traditionally. Each one may only serve ten to fifteen hours per week.

Over the next fifteen years, if the church cannot offset the 50-percent decrease in giving, it can offset the loss of two or three full-time staff pastors with ten part-time or alternative ministers and staff members. These alternative pastors will not be forty-hour-per-week staff members, but their combined efforts more than offset the loss of two "full-time" pastors.

This rough example illustrates the concept of hybrid ministry. The application of the concept will vary across different ministries—just as hybrid auto technology varies across different manufacturers. Like effective automobiles, hybrid ministries cannot be built overnight. But leaders who see the trajectory of the church and who are serious about its survival can consider this as a broad, forward-thinking solution to ministry in the 21st century.

If we begin today, our churches can be prepared when the financial wave of the evangelical recession devastates and surprises unprepared ministries. This step will sound drastic and unnecessary to some optimists. Hybrid auto technology also seemed drastic and unnecessary not long ago. Chrysler and other automakers ignored the new technology. Now those manufacturers are outdated and struggling.

We don't have to wait for the full-fledged crisis. We can begin planning and preparing now. Worship pastors can begin training up worship leaders who do not require full-time pay. Teaching pastors can begin training up teachers who do not require full-time pay. Associate pastors can train up other shepherd-leaders who do not require full-time pay. [2]

Some leaders will be surprised at the number of "lay" brothers and sisters who thrive on making hospital visits and, with time and experience, serve in other pastoral capacities. We all agree that God gifts every member of the body for spiritual service, not just paid pastors (see Romans 12; 1 Corinthians 12; Ephesians 4; and 1 Peter 4). Hybrid ministry compels us to use every gift in the body—not just the ones that fit a full-time salaried position in a 20th-century model.

The Master Engineer's design for this was verbally inspired through an early leader: "And the things you have heard me say in the presence of many witnesses entrust to reliable men who will also be qualified to teach others" (2 Timothy 2:2).

The key is faithful men and women who have found life in Christ. These faithful men and women are the engines of the church. On the heels of the 20th century, we often assume the "faithful" need to be vocational employees of the church. But we do not see that in the New Testament. We do not see it in thriving international churches. I don't believe we will see it in the healthiest 21st-century American churches, either.

In short, the solution is disciples. Not dollars. This alternative energy source was the primary engine of the early church. It is, to this day, the engine of radically growing churches on other continents.

Such an investment into disciples will require some of today's staff members to drop some programs and productions from the 20th-century paradigm in order to train layleaders in the 21st-century paradigm. Developing a hybrid ministry is not easy, but consider these benefits. This paradigm

- prepares your ministry for financial stability during the next fifteen years.
- leads your staff closer to Christ's disciple-training ministry model.
- awakens dormant spiritual gifts in non-staff servant leaders.
- fulfills nonpaid believers who are mature but not yet running in the "good works" God has prepared for them (Ephesians 2:10).
- purifies your leadership team, eliminating "career" church workers.
- attracts true kingdom servants who have no other motive than to serve Christ.
- pleasantly surprises younger Americans, who suspect church staff to be after their money.

Hybrid ministry fits 21st-century culture. When executed well, this model does not just enable the church to plateau in its 20th-century effectiveness, it can actually make the future church more effective at reaching future Americans.

Finally, I do not suggest hybrid ministry because I have master engineered it in my own staff, or even because I've seen it executed perfectly. I suggest it because of massive cultural changes—and more importantly because it's what Christ did. It's what Paul did. And it's what God's Word commands us to do.

I enjoy hiring and leading full-time salaried pastors. They are convenient, fun, and always available. I also enjoy gas-guzzling V-8 engines. They are dragons compared to gas sippers. But the evangelical "fuel crisis" is upon us.

Will we spend the next decade working harder and harder at fundraising—or working harder and harder at disciple making? Leaders with an eye on the long term will, I believe, choose to depend less on dollars and more on disciples. Reprioritizing in this direction is not just strategic. It's also biblical.

The crisis is here. We must plan to do *more* with less. If we don't, we will end up doing *less* with less.

2. Conservation: Avoid debt obligations beyond the next ten years.

"Suppose one of you wants to build a tower. Will he not first sit down and estimate the cost to see if he has enough money to complete it? For if he lays the foundation and is not able to finish it, everyone who sees it will ridicule him, saying, 'This fellow began to build and was not able to finish.'"

Jesus, in Luke 14:28–30

If you knew your salary would be cut in half in the next fifteen years, would you take out a thirty-year mortgage that you can barely afford? I hope not. If you expected your income to decrease, would you set aside additional savings? I hope so.

Even if your ministry is exceptional, it will likely see a decrease in donation revenue per capita over the next fifteen years. This is something we should keep in mind as we prayerfully consider building programs or other debts. Fear of the future must never paralyze us from taking risks in faith. However, we should consider the national trend as we pray over financial risks.

Also, with an awareness of broad pending financial instability, we would do well to conserve resources. Right now—before the donation crisis worsens—is a great time to build up your ministry's reserves and savings. We saw in the Bankrupt chapter that younger givers are not only less generous, they are also less consistent in their giving. That means, barring some sudden change in habits, your ministry's monthly income will become more erratic. At first, the good months may be just as good as they are now, but the bad months will be much worse than they are now. Setting aside a healthy reserve for normal operating expenses will prepare ministries for the lean months in the near future.

If the crisis is as severe as the statistics suggest, then saving alone will not cover the loss indefinitely. Still, well-padded saving could carry your ministry through difficult months or even years. Savings alone are not a sustainable, long-term survival tactic. That's why we also need the paradigm shifts suggested in hybrid ministry, and in the next two tactics: *preparation* and *abandon*.

3. Preparation: Teach mature givers about the recession. Create legacy vehicles, such as bequeathals or ministry trusts, so their gifts can outlive them.

God's work is permanent. It may look especially hard to labor for Christ in this kind of an age but it is possible.

> Pastor Billy Graham, age 23,
> in his September 1944 newsletter to his 75-member
> congregation in Western Springs, Illinois

Joanna had been a trophy wife. Humanly speaking, her best years were behind her. She had tasted wealth and luxury. She had worn the finest clothes, the most expensive perfumes and cosmetics. When Joanna met Jesus as her Savior, she did not think she had much talent or ability to offer almighty God.

Most days, Joanna's husband was too busy for her. His job in the political epicenter required full commitment. He didn't take vacations and would wake in the middle of the night to do his boss's bidding.

Joanna's husband could not give her his time, so he gave her his money. As personal assistant to the wealthiest politician in their country, he had plenty of it. We don't have a record of Joanna teaching classes or conferences. But what she did have, she gave. Joanna is the overlooked and often unspoken financier of Jesus' earthly ministry.

Joanna's husband, Chouza, was personal assistant or "steward" to Herod himself. He kept so busy fulfilling the king's whims that Joanna traveled from city to city with Jesus and his disciples. If Jesus and his disciples stayed at an inn or lodge, it was likely Joanna who paid the bill. When Jesus wasn't providing food miraculously, Joanna was paying for it financially.

God's Word records this in Luke 8:3. We're told that with Jesus and the Twelve were "Joanna the wife of Cuza, the manager of Herod's household; Susanna; and many others. These women were helping to support [Jesus and his disciples] out of their own means." Joanna supported Jesus' ministry financially.

Did God need Joanna's money? In one sense, no. But did God's redemption of humanity include Joanna's money? Yes, it did. God's spiritual plan included Joanna's physical gold and silver. These were the "good works" God had designed for her (Ephesians 2:10). God has a plan now to continue spreading Jesus' gospel message. That plan relies, as it did two thousand years ago, on women and men like Joanna.

We have seen the imminent decline of funds for Christ's work. However, the two oldest generations of United States evangelicals will leave behind more than enough earthly wealth to offset the decline in giving. God's kingdom-work around the world could be "made" or "broken" by trust and bequeathal gifts from these two eldest generations. In this crisis, these generations have the opportunity to leave an eternal legacy like Joanna's.

While Christianity dims in the wealthiest nation in history, the departing generations are presented with an opportunity unlike any in history. Thanks to recent advances in communication and in the spread of evangelical Christianity, the world has never before been so ripe or reachable to Christ's message. We have a greater concentration of evangelical wealth than ever before in history. We have this resource at a time when we also have a window of global peace, during which to spread Christ's Good News.

United States evangelicals now account for less than 20 percent of the global evangelical church. And yet, we hold 80 percent of the worldwide wealth of evangelicals.[3]

Do we really think God gave us four-fifths of His church's wealth so that we could spend it all on ourselves? Economists estimate that our oldest generation passes on about $2 billion of wealth each year, through wills and trusts.[4] One expert believes that in this one generation, Christ's church has "more than enough to fund the fulfillment of the Great Commission."[5] Will we introduce our people to this historic opportunity? Will we lead by example in taking this opportunity?

If we hold 80 percent of the global church's wealth, shouldn't we be sending most of our income to needy Christians around the world? Forward-thinking ministries will lead by example, and will then inform mature believers about the unique and historic moment we have inherited in the United States church.

It was Christ who said, "To whom much is given, much is required" (Luke 12:48). Will the wealthiest Christians in world history leave a legacy like Joanna's, or will we bury these talents, assets, and gifts in the ground? Will American evangelicals hoard our treasures, holding them for ourselves and our heirs—as the wealthy "fool" in Jesus' parable did? Or will we be "rich toward God," for eternal reward (Luke 12:21)?

As evil regroups and spreads—and as the evangelical church struggles at home—American evangelicals have an opportunity to steward Christ's wealth, for His kingdom, in eternal ways.

In Matthew 25:31–40, Jesus sets this scene about His future return as King of Kings:

> "When the Son of Man comes in his glory, and all the angels with him . . . he will separate the people one from another. . . .
>
> Then the King will say to those on his right, 'Come, you who are blessed by my Father; take your inheritance, the kingdom prepared for you since the creation of the world. For I was hungry and you gave me something to eat, I was thirsty and you gave me something

to drink, I was a stranger and you invited me in, I needed clothes and you clothed me, I was sick and you looked after me, I was in prison and you came to visit me.'

Then the righteous will answer him, 'Lord, when did we see you hungry and feed you, or thirsty and give you something to drink? When did we see you a stranger and invite you in, or needing clothes and clothe you? When did we see you sick or in prison and go to visit you?'

The King will reply, 'Truly I tell you, whatever you did for one of the least of these brothers and sisters of mine, you did for me.'"

Apart from radical intervention, United States ministries distributing Christ's Living Water and Bread of Life will be financially crippled in the next fifteen to thirty years. Will we, as intentional leaders, create financial vehicles for our most mature men and women to leave behind resources to continue distributing the eternal life of the Good News?

4. Abandon: Disciple the church in life surrender and biblical tithing.

The evangelical church's stinginess is worst among the youngest. But the crisis is not limited to any one generation. Even with the generous Greatest Generation still among us, "only 3 to 5 percent of Americans who donate money to a church tithe (give a tenth of) their incomes, though many more claim to do so."[6]

The Barna Group has found that 17 percent of evangelicals *claim* to tithe 10 percent of their income to the church, while fewer than 6 percent actually do.[7]

One Christian giving expert estimates, "If members of historically Christian churches in the United States had raised their giving to the Old Testament's minimum standard of giving (10 percent of income) in 2000, an additional $139 billion a year would become available."[8]

The financial crisis is not a shortage of funds. It is a shortage of commitment. We do not believe in tithing or for that matter, generous giving. In Acts 20:35, Paul records Jesus saying, "It is more blessed to give than to receive." But we do not believe Paul, or Jesus. If we did, we would get more excited about giving money away than about hoarding it for ourselves.

More importantly, we do not believe Jesus' simple, direct statement "Where your treasure is, there your heart will be also" (Luke 12:34). If Jesus' claim is true, then the heart of the typical American evangelical is not in Christ's kingdom. Our hearts are in our cars, credit cards, mortgages, and retirement savings.

Ministries that disciple their people into biblical tithing (or into the more radical giving modeled in the New Testament, which appears to be well above 10 percent) can see giving *increase* during the evangelical recession. And the exponential fruit will far exceed dollars. As we disciple our people into biblical stewardship, we are actually helping them place their *hearts* in Christ's kingdom. And once their hearts are in Christ's kingdom, their thoughts and actions, their marriages and families, will follow. As their hearts take root in Christ's kingdom, they will become more committed, more radical disciples.

In this way, the greatest long-term solution to the financial crisis overlaps with the long-term solution to many other "problems" identified in this book—serious reproductive discipleship, in micro relationships. In this case, discipleship would include a leader, probably unpaid, who knows a believer by name and challenges them to more radical obedience in tangible ways—by example first and then in conversation. Only within a framework of committed disciples does biblical generosity make sense.

We have so few givers from the young generations because we have so few radical, abandoned, trained disciples in the young generations. We have so few disciples because we have a shortage of disciple-making leaders in our ministries.

Successful ministries will survive the donation crisis by discipling their people into biblical living and giving. The same ministries will not be as desperate for donations, due to their investment in "hybrid" leaders and layleaders. They will not be mortgaged by earthly assets, because they were cautious about taking on debt. They will also have healthy savings in place, because they saw the crisis on the horizon. And, they may inherit unexpected funds from bequeathal gifts as informed older saints make investments that will outlive them.

Ministries that implement all four of these tactics, with right heart motives, may have more funds than they know what to do with—even as formerly established churches and ministries struggle through the next decades.

Forward-thinking auto manufacturers spent ten years engineering comfortable hybrids that deliver more with less. In the same way, ministries that begin planning now will be doing much more with much less in the coming decades.

11

Healing

How to Slow the Loss of Our People

> Now you are the body of Christ, and each one of you is a part of it.
>
> 1 Corinthians 12:27

In high school I trained as a lifeguard. It was an awkward scene, practicing mouth-to-mouth resuscitation on a rubber dummy in a room full of teenagers. I did swim away with some valuable life lessons, though. I learned the major arteries in the human body:

The carotid—on the neck
The brachial—on the inner bicep
And the femoral—near the hip

These are the big three. Get punctured in one of these arteries, and your life will quickly become, as Solomon said, "a vapor." Also, if you're bleeding out from a wound somewhere else, a trained paramedic could save your life by putting pressure on the big-three artery *above* the wound—thus slowing the flow of leaking blood.

Like most things I learned in lifeguard training, I hoped to never put this knowledge to use. Then, a few summers later, I came across a hit-and-run victim. The man had been riding his bicycle on the shoulder of a four-lane, 50-mile-per-hour road.

Some driver had hit him—tossed him from his bike onto the metal guardrail and then to the ground. The driver didn't bother to stop.

When I jumped out of my Jeep, the bicyclist was lying on his back, cursing in agony, his crushed bike a few yards away. Between his bicep and chest, the man's flannel shirt shined with saturated blood. His body was bleeding out, fast.

Mostly, the blood was flowing from a laceration near his elbow, on his right arm. I was able to put pressure on the higher part of the big-three brachial artery. Given the severity of the bleeding, I used his belt to really clamp down on it. The bleeding slowed. Ten minutes later an ambulance arrived, and the man with the bleeding body lived.

The body of Christ in the United States is, in many ways, like the wounded cyclist I found that day. She is bleeding out. Bleeding to death.

Unfortunately, she has more than one laceration. The leaders who have noticed are scrambling to put pressure on the wounds. Some are targeting young people. Others are targeting the authenticity of our communities. Others, the impersonal corporate feel at some of our churches. We are praying, studying, working harder than ever. And still, the pavement is turning red.

Our ministers are more overwhelmed, strain under higher expectations, and are increasingly burnt out. But the blood continues to spill. We have seen the spattering drops as men and women from our own families and social networks abandon the faith. In chapter 5 (Bleeding), we saw that your own friends and family who've abandoned the faith are not the exceptions. They are the rule.

If we looked *only* at the loss of our young people, we might think our problem is cultural or generational. The solution then would be to become more hip, more relevant, more dogmatic, more _____ (fill in this blank with a national trend that is popular as you read this).

But the problem is far deeper.

Far broader.

And far simpler.

The body is bleeding out because its leaders, its servants, and its people have forgotten how to make disciples as Jesus described and modeled.

We can call it shepherding. We can call it discipleship. We can even call it being relational. What the three have in common is real people dealing with real life, together—and pointing each other to Jesus as they do. What we are failing at is real ministry. Not commercial or mass-marketed events, but real ministry in real lives—the way Paul, Peter, John, and even Jesus did it. We have somehow lost it on a large scale.

To slow the bleeding loss of our young people, we must first reach their parents with authentic, relational discipleship. And to reach the parents, we must first reach their leaders and in many cases, their pastors.

In her book *Almost Christian: What the Faith of Our Teenagers Is Telling the American Church*, Princeton professor Kenda Creasy Dean identified this:

> Since the religious and spiritual choices of American teenagers echo, with astonishing clarity, the religious and spiritual choices of the adults who love them, lackadaisical faith is not young people's issue, but ours. . . . So we must assume that the solution lies not in beefing up congregational youth programs or making worship more "cool" and attractive, but in modeling the kind of mature, passionate faith we say we want young people to have.[1]

We put pressure on the bleeding wounds of the body by resurrecting and rediscovering biblical discipleship. We slow the loss of our people through *personal* training in Christian living, modeled outside of the church service and outside of the church building.

We slow the bleeding of our young people by slowing the bleeding of their parents, many who are physically present but have walked away from the church in their hearts and minds. We slow the bleeding of parents by looking to the higher artery—our leaders and pastors.

To phrase it differently:

We cannot disciple our *children* (so fewer walk away),

until we disciple their *parents*,

which requires discipling their *leaders*,

which requires a *shift in mindset*—a shift away from 20th-century, number-driven models into 21st-century, individual-focused models.

David Kinnaman put it this way: "Some (though not all) ministries have taken cues from the assembly line, doing everything possible to streamline the manufacture of shiny new Jesus-followers, fresh from the factory floor. But disciples cannot be mass-produced. Disciples are handmade, one relationship at a time."[2]

Healing the loss of our people—young and old—will require a shift in how we measure health. George Barna has found that most United States churches measure their success or failure by attendance:

> Our research discovered that when Protestant churches attempt to evaluate their success, one of the primary elements they gauge is attendance. Rather than evaluate spiritual growth, most churches settle for measuring numerical growth, even though a variety of studies have shown there is little correlation between those two metrics.[3]

As with any life-threatening wound, we will begin by applying pressure to the major artery *above* the blood loss. Let's start by seeing what the Bible says about leaders and discipleship.

Healing Our Leaders and Pastors

> The great enemy of the Lord Jesus Christ today is the idea of practical work that has no basis in the New Testament but comes from the systems of the world. This work insists upon endless energy

and activities, but no private life with God. The emphasis is put
on the wrong thing.

Oswald Chambers, *My Utmost for His Highest*

Oswald Chambers stood one hundred years ago in a position
much like ours—on the precipice of a great evangelical recession
in his own country.

Chambers's above statement identified the fault line under
England's Christian recession. The problem was not Darwinism
or socialism. The problem was Christians. Specifically, Christian
leaders who worked their backs crooked and eyes dim, while their
souls slowly lost touch with the Savior.

The same was true of American mainline denomination churches.
We watched them starve themselves to death in the last century. And
now Chambers's description fits many evangelical leaders who—
while holding Scripture high in position—are neglecting it in practice.

Our most dedicated servants are working themselves to collapse
with "endless energy and activities." We are shouldering the business and programs of a late-20th-century church model, wondering
when we or anyone else will have time to do some discipleship or
shepherding.

It has not been our motive, but our outcome has been to neglect Christ's primary and most practical command—to "make
disciples." We saw in the Bleeding chapter that this is a fact. We
are failing at making disciples, whether from new converts or from
children born into the church.

If we want to recover the core of Christ's command—the core
of His church—we must first let go of the extra obligations we
have shouldered onto ourselves.

Leaders are crumbling, often silently and internally, under the
pressures of late-20th-century ministry. Each year pastors suffer
heart attacks, strokes, emotional breakdowns, divorces, and bankruptcies from the strain of this religious system. Many more manage to keep the pressures unknown and internalized.

The Francis A. Schaeffer Institute of Church Leadership Develop-
ment has learned the following from multiple surveys of evangelical
and reformed pastors. These quotes have been edited for brevity:

- 90 percent are frequently fatigued, and worn out on a weekly and even daily basis.
- 71 percent are burned out and battle depression beyond fatigue on a weekly and even a daily basis.
- 81 percent said there was no regular discipleship program or effective effort of mentoring their people or teaching them to deepen their Christian formation at their church.
- 26 percent regularly had personal devotions and felt they were adequately fed spirituality.
- 23 percent felt happy and content on a regular basis with who they are in Christ, in their church, and in their home.[4]

If our pastors and spiritual leaders feel underqualified, overwhelmed, and at times, hypocritical about the demands of the modern church, is it any surprise that our young people are walking away feeling "not good enough," "overwhelmed," and "hypocritical" about their involvement in the church?[5]

It's a simple trickle-down.

If we want to rebuild and restore a culture of discipleship, we have no choice but to release the way American church was done in the 20th century. This begins with pastors, leaders, layleaders, and parents who train up children and teens.

We cannot hold the businesslike 20th-century church model while reclaiming discipleship. We simply do not have enough hands to do both. The demands of the day have delivered to us an either-or ultimatum. A new century insists that we shift our philosophy, out of 20th-century mass-driven measurement models, into 21st-century individual-focused models.

Discipleship Is Not an Option or a Theory

Lest we forget, the bleeding of the body is not theoretical. Our national church body is not bleeding from a skinned knee. A prowling enemy is eating our children. Gnawing on our young men. Isolating them from the flock with pornography, debt, divorce, and slavery. But we have not noticed the missing ones, not as individuals.

The enemy is stalking and destroying our middle-aged men and their sons and daughters—our should-have-been leaders and our would-have-been leaders. We have not noticed the missing hundreds and thousands of them. One by one they quit our churches. Maybe we assume they've gone to another church. Everything must be okay, because the attendance is still growing at *our* church. The giving is still enough to pay the bills for *our* ministry.

We do not notice the wandering sheep. Do not see the wolves lurch onto them, teeth bared. Do not see them collapse defenseless.

We do not smell the stink of death hanging in the enemy's breath. There is blood on his gums, slivers of bone matted into his fur. The blood of our sons, the bones of our daughters. And yet we are busy making excuses. Busy propping up our pride, explaining our methods, assuring others that the statistics have been exaggerated. We are making sure somebody holds this thing together so that everyone gets paid and the lights stay on.

This is an eternal struggle for souls. The demons and angels continue their millennia-long thrashing. Empires are fading pawns in the wrestling for our infants and children, our families and tribes, our churches and cities.

This is the landscape. The war-scape. And we are running Christ's mightiest weapon like a Walmart.

We are trusted by the Chief Shepherd to tend His flock, to nurture His bride, to train His warriors. Nobody will do it for us if we get it wrong. And we are taking management tips from Subway, McDonald's, and Disney.

The simple but demanding discipleship I'm suggesting can be argued *against* a thousand different ways. It is, I know, too simple. On the other hand, it is (I know) too difficult. How heated and passionate we become when defending our complacency, our apathy toward Christ's discipleship mandate.

Our documented failure at Jesus' style of leadership can be rationalized, explained away, even applauded. We have gotten so much *better* at church than Jesus of Nazareth. We're more sophisticated, better organized, better funded. And look how full our parking lots are!

What if Jesus came to speak in some of our staff meetings, board meetings, or annual meetings? We would look at each other, thinking but not saying, *How naïve Jesus is. How little He knows about running a successful ministry in this day and age.*

We simply do not have time to do ministry the way Jesus would. He doesn't understand how many other things vie for our attention.

But if we will be still for a moment . . . if we will open our ears to God's Spirit . . . if we will watch our gentle Savior move among the Galilean peasants . . . watch His unsettled pace, His patient redirecting of the Twelve, again and again. Remember His unnoticed escapes and absences into prayer.

If we will stop explaining away His life and His words, we will see that we have, in many cases, neglected the simple, unremarkable work of the kingdom. We have abandoned the work He modeled for three years because we have been too busy with remarkable, demanding, measurable efforts.

Releasing Leaders From Human Expectations

I'm told that pastors aren't supposed to have favorites. But I do. Bruce, a 6-foot, 4-inch tree of a man, will always be among mine.

Bruce's gentle presence has a way of suspending you when you're spiritually weak. Some days he'll look in your eyes, pause, and slowly say, "Do you know that God is proud of you?" Or, "How are you feeling God's love today?" Then he waits for you to answer.

Walk into Bruce's office at Hometown Transmission, and you will see a car's color-coded transmission cut in half. You'll see some Scripture verses. And then you'll see a quote on a poster. I call it a Bruce-ism: "Energy Flows Where Attention Goes."

Here's the point: Whatever you focus on, that person or problem will get your energy. So direct your attention intentionally. In so doing, you will also direct your energy.

This Bruce-ism sums up why we are where we are today in the United States church. We have been so attentive to numbers, among other things, that we have not noticed the body's bleeding from various wounds. We have focused on so many other good things that we have not focused on genuine relational discipleship.

This is not because we think discipleship is unimportant. Any Christian leader will tell you it is. Primary. Central. Of undeniable, utmost importance. But examine the calendar, the weekly routine of us pastors and leaders, and you won't find much room for relational discipleship. Not the sort modeled by Jesus.

We have neglected it. Not because we don't believe in it. But because the energy has been flowing where our attention has been going—programs, budgets, productions, emergencies, firefighting, advertising, events, vision catching, vision casting. The list continues and varies by ministry: hiring, blogging, planning, teaching, and so forth.

The "tyranny of the urgent" has overtaken us. The late-20th-century church model, in many applications, requires so much energy and attention that little to nothing is left for anything else, including discipleship. It is an unintended consequence of our misdirected attention.

We cannot reclaim Christlike and Pauline discipleship if we do not let go of these energy-draining, attention-demanding expectations. In this sense, our bleeding begins at "the top." It begins with the attention of our senior and CEO leaders—a group to which I belong and for which my heart breaks.

The younger generation is bleeding out visibly. But a silent wound is bloodletting internally, quietly, secretly. Pastors and leaders hide bruises under their smiles. Their legs burn as they carry growing pressures and fears. If leaders confess their loss of heart and life, they could lose their jobs, or at least the respect needed to do them. And so they bleed in secret.

Contemporary pastors and leaders carry a weight of criticism and pressure that non-pastors simply cannot imagine. I learned this as a young boy. Some of my friends' parents spent the drive home from church—and a good portion of lunch—criticizing their shepherds. Perhaps they thought I was too young to be listening. I was listening.

I couldn't understand why they criticized. I never once heard my dad, a senior pastor of about eight hundred, criticize his people. I only saw him work seven-day weeks to love them.

Christians have been criticizing their ministers since the 1st century. This we know from Paul's encouragement to Pastor

Timothy—that he should tune out the critics in his congregation and tune in to his gifting, calling, heritage, and support network.

It has always been difficult to be a pastor. But it has probably never been more difficult than it is *right now*. A hundred years ago, pastors were expected to spend time in God's Word, to pray, to visit the sick, to be friendly, and to preach. Fifty years ago, pastors were expected to do all this, but also with an advanced seminary degree, reasonable people skills, and a Sunday school class.

In the late 20th century, additional expectations accumulated. The pastor was to be

- an aggressive entrepreneur and tender people person,
- a visionary and someone who has time to talk,
- an executive and a finance manager,
- a staff manager, elder, or deacon manager,
- a volunteer coordinator,
- an overseer of political factions within the church.

Now, pastors are expected (or expect themselves) to carry all the above duties while also

- consistently producing entertaining, biblical, podcast-quality messages,
- being missional and relational in the community,
- networking through social media,
- modeling a radical lifestyle of following Christ with passion.

The pastor is expected to do all this while spending hours in prayer and Bible study, and of course, ministering first to his family.

Many leaders are to do all this with a decreasing budget and a decreasing staff. I found a good laugh—and a bit of truth—in this description of an ideal pastor, emailed to me by a fun-loving church member. I'll paraphrase for you:

The perfect pastor works twelve-hour days, seven days a week, and is always rested and available.

He wears fine clothes and is also a janitor.

He earns less than the average congregant, and he buys good
books, gives generously, and provides for his family.

He is always out visiting the sick, needy, and elderly, and he
is always waiting in his office if you walk in with an urgent
need.

He speaks the truth boldly, but he never offends anybody.

Whether old-school expectations like these or new-school expectations of hipness and "relevance," the web of human expectations
can choke any Christian leader, of any age, in any organization.
Release from these human pressures comes from only one place—
from entering God's presence and, once there, from fearing Him
more than man.[6] Indeed, "Where the Spirit of the Lord is, there is
freedom" (2 Corinthians 3:17).

Leaders who struggle under the burden of expectations or the
weight of people-pleasing can unload those burdens in exchange
for this freedom: "If I were still living to please men, I would not
be the servant of Christ" (Galatians 1:10).

We leaders are, at times, the most desperate of all people for
Christ's gentle invitation to "come to me" and exchange our burdens for His (Matthew 11:28).

This exchange is needed individually and nationally, if we are
to transition into 21st-century ministry. We cannot reclaim God's
simple expectations until we break free from the additional bur-
densome demands of the last decades.

If you're like me, you have shouldered these expectations, perhaps unawares. If we want to recover God's heart for His body,
if we want to disciple as Christ discipled, and if we want to rediscover the Chief Shepherd's love for His sheep, we must release
expectations that aren't from Him. Often, we ourselves have invited
these expectations into our hearts, likely from insecurity, pride,
or emotional need.

We must be unafraid of disappointing people, including ourselves, because we fear God more. After all, if we teach, we will
receive a stricter judgment from *Him* (James 3:1). Shouldn't we
fear His judgment more than we fear a lack of growth in our
weekend attendance?

And the more souls we have in our care, the more souls we will be held directly accountable for *to Him* (Hebrews 13:17). Shouldn't we fear the imminent accounting for each lamb more than we fear what others think of our success or failure by human measures?

Let us recommit ourselves to *His* priorities, no matter the cost— that we might adjust our five-year plans, our one-year goals, and our daily calendars.

My prayer is that this chapter is not an obligation for leaders, not another to-do on the too-tall mountain of pastor tasks. My hope is that this chapter grants permission to those whose hearts have been quietly telling them that it's more about the people and less about the programs. More about soul-communion with God and less about the calendar. Let your faith in Christ's example move that mountain of tasks into the sea of forgetfulness.

Give yourself permission to abandon some 20th-century expectations, in order to recapture your calling, your passion, and your shepherd's heart.

In God's priorities for His people, we find rest and simplicity. Every spiritual leader of every century has but three callings:[7]

- Love God
- Love God's Word
- Love God's people

A successful day accomplishes nothing more than these three callings. If, like me, you wake many mornings to a cold heart that does not love God, His people, or His Word, there is still hope. Our Redeemer actually gives the spiritual energy for these callings. It is, as Paul says, "All [God's] energy, which so powerfully works in me" (Colossians 1:29).

As we love God personally, inviting Him to inject His love into the cavities of our hearts, His energy works powerfully through our weaknesses. But we must take time to acknowledge and expose those weaknesses to Him. The Vine grows through the yielding cracks in our self-dependence,[8] and He bears the fruit.

Because this book is not a primer for pastoral ministry, I will skip to the third of these three calls—loving God's people. This cannot be done without a love for God himself and His Word. *But a missing pastoral love for our individual people is the highest, most gaping wound of our bleeding body. So we will focus on this timeless calling.*

If we will recover a biblical love for God's people as individuals, the bleeding will slow in our ministries.

Loving God's People

> When he saw the crowds, he had compassion on them, because they were harassed and helpless, like sheep without a shepherd.
>
> Matthew 9:36

Phoenix Seminary professor Dr. John DelHousaye taught me that brilliant men can also be humble. I'll never forget the Greek class when he explained the word *compassion* in the above verse.

We get our English word "spleen" from the Greek word *splagxnon*, or "compassion" used in this verse. In other words, Jesus' stomach turned. His insides twisted in emptiness. Why? Because He looked at the people He loved and saw they were helpless. They were scattered. They were not led, fed, or protected as individuals.

Unfortunately, if Jesus walked into the lobbies, coffee shops, and parking lots of many evangelical churches today, He could say the exact same thing. His people are "like sheep without a shepherd."

The American church has traded shepherding—the highest call of a pastor—for management. In the worst cases, we have traded it for showmanship and social engineering.

We have cut spiritual corners with human scissors. Why is it that thirty or forty years ago, a typical evangelical had a pastor who knew him or her by name? And why is it that now many don't have such a pastor?

There was a time when a pastor could visit you in your home, at the hospital, at your child's graduation. He could notice if you were missing on a given Sunday.

Has our number exploded so that there are not enough pastors to go around? We saw in the Sputtering and Bleeding chapters that this is not the case. Evangelicals have shrunk as a percentage of the population. No, the number of evangelicals has not boomed. We have just become more centralized in fewer, larger churches that produce a better Sunday performance. Not always, but too often, the larger crowd and better performance have cost us in our shepherding of individuals.

The change has come in philosophy of ministry. Simple discipleship and care for the sheep have been lost in many ministries. Somewhere along the way they got painted over in the constant struggle for progress, for more, for bigger and better.

In some contexts, the business model of the church does not allow "pastors" room to do true pastoral care. In other contexts, one committed shepherd-pastor is attempting to do all the shepherding in a large flock, without time or space to reproduce other leaders through discipleship. As the flock grows, one shepherd cannot touch all the sheep—not even within a subministry like youth, young adults, or an additional venue.

More and more, the most "successful" of our leaders won't touch actual shepherding—won't get their hands in the mud, their fingers in the wounds, their hearts in the lives of the people. That priority trickles down through staff and layleaders to parents and kids.

Worse yet, that priority contradicts what Jesus identified as the epitome and essence of ministry in *His* kingdom. The epitome of our Teacher and Lord was Him on His knees, arms dripping, mud under His fingernails, hands scrubbing 120 toenails, His fingers gently washing each toe, including the ten that propelled Judas to His crucifiers.[9]

After this visual lesson, Jesus explained, "No servant is greater than his master, nor is a messenger greater than the one who sent him" (John 13:16). Today we have too many servants who are too great to serve as Jesus did.

God has been calling His leaders "shepherds" for thousands of years. He put it this way to the prophet Ezekiel:

> This is what the Sovereign Lord says: Woe to the shepherds of Israel who only take care of themselves! Should not shepherds take care

of the flock? . . . You do not take care of the flock. You have not
strengthened the weak or healed the sick or bound up the injured.
You have not brought back the strays or searched for the lost. . . .
My sheep wandered over all the mountains and on every high hill.
They were scattered over the whole earth, and no one searched or
looked for them.

Ezekiel 34:2–6

In case you missed it, "My sheep wandered . . . and no one
searched or looked for them."

In contrast to these career religious leaders, God describes
himself to Isaiah as one who "tends his flock like a shepherd: He
gathers the lambs in his arms and carries them close to his heart;
he gently leads those that have young" (Isaiah 40:11).

God's choice analogy for leadership continues into the New
Testament. Consider that the Greek word for *shepherd* is only
translated "pastor" one time in mainstream translations.[10] The
other sixteen uses clearly mean a herder of the sheep—one who
lives among the sheep, who gives his life to care for them, feed
them, lead them to water, bind up their wounds, protect them
from wolves, carry them when they are weak, and seek them
when they wander.

Jesus used this word *shepherd*, the origin of our word "pastor,"
to refer to himself and His servants. Trace it through the gospels
and see the contrast between His ideas of shepherding and our
ideas of what a "pastor" does today.[11]

It is sad to look around the American church and see how many
"pastors" we have in title, but how few shepherds. How many who
carry the name "pastor" and work at modern traditions. How few
true shepherds we have—as Jesus used the word.

In 2009, the Leadership Network surveyed megachurch pastors,
asking them to define their job. Here are their responses:

81% Preacher-teacher
51% Directional leader
33% Visionary
16% Pastor[12]

Obviously, one pastor cannot touch every sheep in a church of thousands—or even of hundreds. In the next section we will answer how pastors of large ministries can still be shepherds. The point here is that we cannot reclaim discipleship without touching the sheep. And it's hard to justify avoiding the sheep when we see that Jesus calls His leaders shepherds.

If our leaders will touch the sheep again, love the sheep again, then we can reclaim discipleship the way Jesus did it. And if we will reclaim discipleship, then we can train parents, who can in turn train their children. This is the pressure that must be applied at the major artery in order to slow the bleeding of the United States church.

When the People Are Too Many to Love

Keep watch over yourselves and all the flock of which the Holy Spirit has made you overseers. Be shepherds of the church of God, which he bought with his own blood.

Acts 20:28

We have not shepherded individuals. And we cannot disciple those we are not shepherding. Our failure here is the bloodiest. This single neglect results in many more losses downstream from the artery, including the loss of our youth.

Only you can determine how to resurrect discipleship and shepherding in your ministry. That is your calling. My calling is to proclaim that if we do not resurrect discipleship and shepherding across United States evangelical churches, our body will continue bleeding out.

We can start, some of us, this very moment—by repenting on our knees and by asking God to restore His heart for His sheep. Let's learn discipleship from the One who created it, the One who commands it, the Good Shepherd.

After Jesus looked on the crowds and had compassion, because they were "without a shepherd," in the same passage, Jesus gives His solution to the problem. He says to pray for laborers (Matthew 9:38). We often filter this verse through an evangelism sieve. We hear "pray for laborers" and think of missionaries or vocational "pastors."

That's not what Jesus was talking about. Look at the previous verses. Jesus isn't talking about soul winners or tribal missionaries here. He's talking about shepherds for scattered sheep.

Not converters, but caretakers.

Not lead pastors, but laborers.

Not sheep managers, but shepherds.

And here's where discipleship begins—in the search for laborers. Jesus didn't stop at praying for laborers. He searched for them, found them, challenged them to be disciples, and then trained the committed for service.

Not by the hundreds.

But rather, one by one.

He only trained one dozen in His whole ministry.

He trained twelve for three intense years, and eleven turned out swimmingly. To love all of our people, we must start as Jesus and Paul did—by investing in a small team of "faithful" ones "who will teach others also" (2 Timothy 2:2).

That is, we love more of them by focusing on a few of the faithful. We train the few to love others, who will in turn love and train others. A Christlike leader is constantly praying for more laborers, spotting them, recruiting them, training them, and unleashing them to be reproductive.

A Christlike leader is not personally training hundreds or thousands at once. (Such is an attempt to do more than God himself did.) The Christlike leader may teach groups of thousands, as Jesus and Paul did, but the core of his or her ministry is recruiting and training leaders, by the dozen or so. (Remember, when Jesus gave the iconic picture of ministry—the washing of the disciples' feet—the lesson was for His core twelve, not for the thousands who would have eagerly gathered to hear Jesus teach the lesson in the temple.)

In this sense, the Christlike leader believes that smaller is bigger, that we love the multitudes by training the few. We train the few to train a few more, so that in time, every sheep has a shepherd.

This leaves room for huge congregations where small-team training is happening. This also leaves room for the various spiritual gifts of the body. In our late-20th-century model, many of our pastors are most gifted in administration and/or teaching, not shepherding. Some of our strongest teachers and leaders are the weakest at relationships.

That's okay. Such leaders should not ignore their God-given call to teach and organize the masses, but no matter how gifted any of us are, we are not exempt from discipleship. Such senior, teaching, and executive pastors can and must train small teams of future leaders, even while they lead, teach, or administer as unto the Lord.

Too often, our most gifted teaching pastors leave a leadership vacuum when they exit a ministry. In secular terms, Jim Collins calls these dynamic personalities Level 4 Leaders. They are "the genius with a thousand helpers," he says. While they helm the ship, everything goes great . . . until they leave. Things fall apart after their departure, because they have not raised up replacements. If anyone could have been a genius with a thousand helpers, it was Jesus. But He did not leave a massive organization that couldn't operate without Him. He left eleven trained disciples who *could* operate without Him.

It says something about our culture of discipleship when many of our "best" leaders, after ten to thirty years in a church, have not trained up one single disciple to take their place. Ministry, in Jesus' view, was never a solo pursuit. Jesus served among His disciples and asked them to be present with Him in times of great testing, like the garden of Gethsemane. When Jesus sent His disciples out, it was in pairs, not as individuals (Mark 6:7).

The apostle Paul, like Jesus, was training up a handful of replacements within his first years of ministry. Paul's focus was not the crowds of hundreds and thousands that he taught. His focus was his Timothys, Tituses, and Philemons.

In addition to Jesus' and Paul's examples, personal shepherding was also Christ's final command to the "rock" on which He built the church. Peter had a personality and exceptional gifting probably like some of our more dynamic but less relational teachers and visionaries. Reading Peter's epistles, though, we sense that he never forgot Jesus' final commands to him: If you love me, "feed my sheep" and "take care of my sheep" (John 21:15–18).

Leaders need not be personally discipling hundreds of people, but they had better be training a small team of future leaders, as Jesus and Paul did. If these disciples turn around and train others, the trickle-down will slow the bleeding of the body. Healthy recoveries take time. Holistic discipleship will spread through the cultures of our organizations, if we will devote attention and energy to it.

If we will let go of 20th-century expectations and return to Christ in this one way, it will slow the internal bleeding of our paid leaders, of our unpaid leaders, and of our parents. As a result, in time, it will slow the loss of our children.

This leaves room for counselors, pastoral pastors, and others who are most gifted at binding up wounds, counseling, crying, and praying with dozens of sheep. In fact, it launches the latent gifts of mercy, hospitality, and encouragement that lie dormant in many of our laypeople. It trains up—by the dozen—many more shepherds to tend the flock, so that, eventually, every sheep in the fold has at least one shepherd who knows him or her by name (even if that shepherd does not draw a paycheck from the church).

Leaders who know that relational discipleship is not a personal strength should build a staff to complement their weakness. In this way, the leader's area of weakness does not deform the entire ministry.

Jesus taught thousands. Paul, Barnabas, and the apostles "taught great numbers of people," certainly in the thousands (Acts 2:41; 11:26). But their daily focus was simple: developing individual leaders and small leadership teams. They trained these faithful ones, *not in event production*, but in caring for and training dozens of other individuals.

Hundreds followed Jesus, but He was possessive and intentional about His energy and time. He saved His best energy not for marketing or planning, not even for teaching. He saved His best for investing in the Twelve and for praying.

Jesus invested heavily in a core of future leaders. So did Paul. This is the biblical model of shepherding—the training of under-shepherds. Lead pastors and ministry CEOs need not know every single sheep. But we'd better know a core of under-shepherds who do know the sheep—and who lead and feed the sheep.

As with the bleeding bicyclist I found on the side of the road, we heal the bleeding body by first applying pressure to the major artery *above* the obvious wound.

It will take time, and it will mean abandoning many 20th-century priorities, but if we leaders will shepherd and train "faithful" leaders, and if those leaders will duplicate what they learn, then the healing will, in time, reach the parents and youth volunteers who disciple our teens.

By the Holy Spirit's power and with God's grace, you can slow the bleeding of the body as you follow Jesus in this simple way.

Pray for laborers.

Find them.

Train them.

Aside from your one primary gifting, release whatever other tasks hinder you from obeying Jesus in this simple mandate. This is *Christ's* remedy to our blood loss. *His* spoken solution for our scattered sheep.

12

Re-Igniting

How to Restart the Engine of Evangelism

Those who had been scattered preached the word wherever they went.

Acts 8:4

Have you seen the recent Mormon television commercials? Commonly, they profile some non-Mormon-looking person—usually an athlete, artist, or ethnic minority who exudes uber-coolness. They don't look anything like the stereotypical Mormon. They don't say anything about religion. They seem like someone you'd be proud to know. The commercials end with the same alarming revelation: "My name is so-and-so (pause). And I'm a Mormon."

Talk about a shocker. I don't know if these commercials convince anyone to convert to Mormonism or not. But they can't be bad for the group's image.

More than once I have caught myself wishing, *Oh that we evangelicals could work together to produce something so simple and mainstream and persuasive—because we have even cooler people.*

I know that's an immature impulse. I know it's comparative and short of spiritual. As I've reflected on this, I've concluded that the desire isn't bad. It's the methodology that's skewed.

In chapter 8, we saw that Christ does indeed want His people to be known for their GOOD-ness. However, His method is not a media campaign. His method is each individual believer embracing their identity as a breathing, walking billboard, modeling life in Christ. What's true about the GOOD-ness is equally true about the GOOD NEWS. God's plan for spreading the gospel is not a national media campaign. It is, according to His Word, every individual believer proclaiming the message, wherever we go (Acts 1:8).

In this sense, we can have at least 22 million convincing advertisements playing multiple times a day, in thousands of media markets across the United States.

In the Sputtering chapter, we saw that the engine of evangelism has stalled in the United States church. Our rate of new converts is not keeping pace with population growth. Each ensuing generation of Americans has fewer evangelicals than the previous generation. We now see that God's solution, His method for *re-igniting* the engine of evangelism, is not a national media campaign. It's not even a few high-powered evangelists, as great as that would be. God's solution requires zero dollars in funding and 100 percent in commitment.

His solution, we will see, is the church. That is, every individual follower of Christ relearning what it is to share the Good News with their neighbors, coworkers, family members, and friends. This is the only fuel combustible enough to re-ignite the stalled engine of evangelism in the United States.

Mass evangelism has always played a role in God's spread of His message. In the United States, Billy Graham's crusades likely marked the peak of mass evangelism. We can pray for more such evangelists going forward. But we cannot rely on a handful of big hitters to get the job done for the entire United States. As we'll see, God did use mass evangelism to build the New Testament church, but He primarily grew the church through thousands of individual believers—each one radically committed to Christ.

Christ calls each of us to "go and make disciples." Our greatest potential for reaching the lost is not a celebrity leader, but millions of less-known everyday believers. There's a recent business term for this principle. It's called the "Long Tail." Allow me to explain.

Understanding the Long Tail

The 21st century is just getting started, but we've already seen some game-changing bankruptcies—Blockbuster and Borders, to name two. Forces greater than the recession tackled these behemoths. The Long Tail is one of those forces.

Four years before Blockbuster Video declared bankruptcy, *Wired Magazine* editor Chris Anderson wrote his book *The Long Tail*. In it, Anderson described a 21st-century phenomenon that many ministries still don't understand. Here's the gist of it.

Anderson refers to big hits in the retail market as "the head" of the sales curve. In media, this includes bestselling authors like John Grisham and Stephen King, rock stars like Madonna and Coldplay, or blockbuster films like *Pirates of the Caribbean* and *Jurassic Park*. These are "the head" of the market, the high-volume big hitters. In the 20th century, companies could make money by focusing exclusively on these big hits and ignoring everything else.

Blockbuster didn't need to stock every movie—just bestselling new releases. Borders didn't need to stock every book—just the top few percent of sellers. This model worked great—right up to the late 1990s. Today, however, it's a model for bankruptcy.

Viewed as a graph of sales volume, the "head" of bestsellers slopes downward. As you move away from the head, the sales decrease. There's a very short "neck" of C-list type products. And then there's a very long tail, stretching away from the head.

The Long Tail represents the thousands of movies, books, and songs that hardly sell. But when all those thousands of items are combined they generate just as much revenue as big hits in the head. The mass (or profit) of the many small sellers in the tail is actually the same as the mass (or profit) of the few big sellers in the head.

To visualize, picture a medieval dragon from a side, profile view. The mass in the muscular neck and head are about the same volume as the mass in the powerful long tail. Similarly, the money to be made in all the little non-hits is about the same as the money to be made in the few big hits in the neck and head.

Anderson observed that if a company could learn to sell all the products in the tail, it would excel in the 21st century. And that is exactly what Netflix, Amazon, iTunes, and other thriving young brands have done. They've learned to sell the tail and not rely exclusively on the big hits. They operate knowing there's more money in the combined volume of all the non-hits than in just the hits. (This is why you see so many non-hit movies you've never heard of listed on Netflix.) Netflix's ownership of the Long Tail obliterated Blockbuster's outdated head-dependent model.

While Borders has gone bankrupt, Amazon has capitalized on the Long Tail of the book market. Netflix, Amazon, and iTunes are so good at selling the products in the Long Tail that they've incidentally become the go-to destinations for purchasing best-sellers from the head as well. Whether you're looking for a niche product or a mainstream bestseller, you know these companies will have what you're looking for.

In a sense, Facebook, Google, and Wikipedia are also capitalizing on the Long Tail—in people and information. Instead of bringing us news about a few celebrities, as some struggling publications do, Facebook brings us news from all the non-famous people whom we care about—people from the Long Tail of society. And Google gives us access to the Long Tail of information. Instead of telling us what information in the head to care about, as struggling print newspapers do, Google gives direct access to all the information in the Long Tail—including lots of info that may not be bestselling, but appeals to us individually. Wikipedia offers tens of thousands more entries than old print encyclopedias. It's a lot of Long Tail information.

How does the Long Tail relate to evangelism? Just like industry, the 20th-century model for evangelism in the United States relied on the head, big hitters like Billy Graham. Locally, we relied on inviting folks to big events like Christmas or Easter outreaches. That used to be a fine model, but it's grossly outdated because it ignores the Long Tail, the millions of other "non-hit" evangelical Christians. It ignores us normal people—and God's plan to use all His people.

In business, relying solely on the head these days demonstrates ignorance about how culture has changed—how people are more individual, more selective, less of a herd, and exponentially more informed. In ministry, so long as we look exclusively to big names or even local big-hit events to get evangelism done, we will be irrelevant and outdated.

Even within the local context, most evangelical churches still rely primarily on a local head-based model for evangelism. The seeker approach (expecting an unbeliever to attend a church or evangelistic event) draws people to the head—big events. This worked in the 1900s, because of the somewhat-Christian culture that many Americans had grown up in. It will work less and less in a post–baby boomer era, because fewer Americans will have any sort of Christian lens. Missions expert Ed Stetzer identifies this change in culture—and the church's failure to notice it—as one of the most important issues facing United States evangelicalism today:

> Evangelicals must learn to navigate what I call a "post-seeker context. . . ." [C]hurches that once targeted seekers from the Boomer generation are finding that large portions of subsequent generations do not have the same religious memory. . . . For evangelicals to reach [genuine spiritual] seekers in the decade ahead, they will need to develop new models and other means of communication to deliver our message into the cultural destination of an increasingly post-seeker context. When religious memory is gone, we can no longer rely on those outside of the faith to be interested in what it means to be inside of the faith.[1]

In broad terms, the American seeker model started well before the 1900s, in the earlier American revivals. This "head," or event-based evangelism, worked great in a culture where businesses shut down on Sundays, where students prayed in public schools, where church buildings hosted civic events, and where adults remembered a church-centric childhood. Seeker, event-based evangelism probably culminated in the late 1900s. While it still serves a purpose in some communities, it is a cultural relic that will prove less and less fruitful in most applications.[2]

Like thriving, forward-thinking businesses, our ministries must shift away from the 20th-century big-hit model and embrace the 21st-century individual-focused model. We could call this the Long Tail of evangelism—millions of individual believers functioning as evangelists in their own lives. Each individual evangelical will not be winning hundreds or thousands to Christ. But if each one wins just one, then the 22 million of us in the Long Tail can win more than any one evangelist.

As proof, consider this. The Institute for American Church Growth asked 10,000 people: "What was responsible for your coming to Christ and this church?" The answers were:

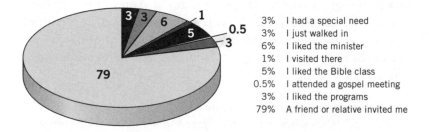

3%	I had a special need
3%	I just walked in
6%	I liked the minister
1%	I visited there
5%	I liked the Bible class
0.5%	I attended a gospel meeting
3%	I liked the programs
79%	A friend or relative invited me

The vast majority of unbelieving Americans do not come to Christ—or to a church—because of a big-hitter. They come because of a friend or relative. They come because of their own unique connection to the Long Tail.

Embracing the Long Tail does not require us to decapitate the head. Indeed, as mentioned earlier, Netflix, Amazon, and iTunes have excelled by offering the bestsellers in the head, as well as all the small sellers in the Tail.

We need gifted evangelists and big-event outreaches more than ever. But those alone cannot turn the seized cylinders in the engine of evangelism. In the 21st century, we need the entire body of Christ to take evangelism seriously, as it did in the 1st century. Acts 8:4 tells us, "Those who had been scattered preached the word wherever they went." Note that this was not just the apostles. It was all of them. This is how the church exploded exponentially—because the Long Tail was directly and personally proclaiming. They were not silently modeling or occasionally inviting. Individuals in the Long Tail "preached the word wherever they went."

To successfully convert unbelievers today, the church must capitalize on the untapped potential of individual non-celebrity Christians. This Long Tail of "normal" believers is the secret to restarting our evangelism engine. It is, incidentally, also what Jesus prescribed.

The Long Tail Is Biblical

Not only is the Long Tail practical. Not only does it understand today's times and trends. It is also biblical.

Even when the church had miracle-working apostles healing the blind and raising the dead, the evangelism engine did not run solely on big-hitter evangelists. Yes, the New Testament church enjoyed moments when 3,000 or 5,000 came to Christ after a single sermon, as in Acts 2:41 and 4:4. That's definitely the head—the bestselling, big-hitting impact of a gifted preacher or evangelist. Such evangelism is clearly a biblical part of God's plan. But it's not the only part of the plan.

The New Testament church also relied on the Long Tail—the thousands of individual ministers of the gospel:

> Now those who had been scattered by the persecution in connec-
> tion with Stephen traveled . . . telling the message. . . . The Lord's
> hand was with them, and a great number of people believed and
> turned to the Lord.
>
> Acts 11:19–21

> "But you will receive power when the Holy Spirit comes on you;
> and you will be my witnesses in Jerusalem, and in all Judea and
> Samaria, and to the ends of the earth."
>
> Acts 1:8

Some will have a special spiritual gift of evangelism. However, Acts 1:8 clearly instructs that regardless of our specific spiritual gift, we are each to be active "witnesses," just as we are all to "make disciples." Nobody in the Acts church was on the sidelines when it came to witnessing or disciple-making.

Similarly, this mandate in 1 Peter is given (decades later) to all individual believers—in this case a motley assortment of Christians scattered over a broad cluster of areas (see 1 Peter 1:1):

> But in your hearts set apart Christ as Lord. Always be prepared to give an answer to everyone who asks you to give the reason for the hope that you have. But do this with gentleness and respect.
>
> 1 Peter 3:15

The apostle Peter says all believers—of all ages, incomes, spiritual gifts, genders, and so forth—must "always be prepared to give an answer." Not always prepared to invite to an event, though that's profitable. Not always living a silent example, though that's also important. But every believer is to be "always prepared" to speak with their mouth and explain the Good News behind the goodness of their life.

Epaphras—a fairly unknown disciple—was one of us normal folks from the Long Tail. He led a few people to the Lord in the city of Colossi. Because Epaphras was faithful, God built a church in Colossi, and today we enjoy Paul's letter to that church—Colossians.

Our evangelism engine is not sputtering for lack of big events. Our evangelism engine is sputtering because it's low on the fuel of the Long Tail. It's low on individual believers verbally explaining the gospel, from the platform of a life that earns the right to speak. Our struggling evangelism engine indicates our apathy toward classic evangelical passages like these, below. Incidentally, these are the sort of verses that, in many evangelical circles, used to be memorized widely by laypeople:

> "In the same way, I tell you, there is rejoicing in the presence of the angels of God over one sinner who repents."
>
> Luke 15:10

> He who wins souls is wise.
>
> Proverbs 11:30

For Christ's love compels us, because we are convinced that one
died for all, and therefore all died.

2 Corinthians 5:14

He answered, "Then I beg you, father, send Lazarus to my father's
house, for I have five brothers. Let him warn them, so that they will
not also come to this place of torment."

Luke 16:27–28

It was normal in the New Testament for converts to be unable
to restrain themselves from telling their friends and family about
Jesus. In fact, many of the earliest believers personally brought
their family members to faith in Christ. It seems this was the norm,
and not the exception.

Take Andrew, for example:

The first thing Andrew did was to find his brother Simon and tell
him, "We have found the Messiah."

John 1:41

Personal evangelism saturated the New Testament church culture:

- Matthew brought many of his friends to meet Jesus. (Mark
  2:13–15)
- Cornelius, as he was seeking Christ, brought "his relatives
  and close friends" to hear the gospel. And they believed. (Acts
  10:24, 44)
- When the Lord opened Lydia's heart to the Good News, she
  brought all "the members of her household" to salvation,
  too. (Acts 16:15)
- Timothy, Paul's disciple and protégé, was brought to faith
  by the personal evangelism of his mother and grandmother.
  (2 Timothy 1:5)
- The Ethiopian eunuch heard the gospel in a one-on-one conversation (Acts 8:26–40), as did multiple prison guards, including the Philippian jailer (Acts 16:31) and later the "whole

palace guard" (Philippians 1:13) as well as many in "Caesar's household" (Philippians 4:22).

In the New Testament, disciples of all sorts were speaking up as personal and active witnesses for Jesus Christ. Many in our evangelical churches today do not believe that they are gifted to do this—or even called to do it. Many of them have never seen what it looks like out on the street, in the office, or over the neighborhood fence.

Of course, only a minority of believers will have the spiritual gift of evangelism (Acts 21:8 and Ephesians 4:11). But we are all—without exception—called to "go and make disciples." And in case we missed it, God calls us to "be *my* witnesses." We have settled for the majority of our people being silent supporters but not proclaimers, not witnesses in the sense that the New Testament used the word—ones who testify to what we have seen Christ do. Just as those without the gift of giving still give, and those without the gift of mercy still show mercy, those of us without the gift of evangelism are still called to be witnesses and make disciples.

However, the present climate in many evangelical churches is such that even if someone has the gift of evangelism, it may sit dormant for a lifetime, because they are rarely encouraged or challenged to step out and share Christ verbally. Personal evangelism is not often applauded or explained, let alone modeled in real life or in discipleship relationships. Unfortunately, in many of our churches, we have neglected the gifts in the Long Tail. This is especially true of evangelism.

When we attempt to emphasize personal evangelism, it often comes across as an impossible request—because we have not discipled our people into lifestyles that draw the curiosity of unbelievers (1 Peter 3:15).

In his book *The Gospel and Personal Evangelism*, Mark Dever writes:

[W]hen we read the New Testament, we don't read of the call to evangelism being limited to Paul, or even to the apostles. It was Jesus himself, in his final commission to his disciples who taught . . .

"Therefore go and make disciples. . . ." . . . According to the Bible, all believers have received this commission.[3]

Dever then quotes John Stott's 1949 book, *Personal Evangelism.*

[The Great Commission] . . . is binding upon every member of the whole church. . . . Every Christian is called to be a witness to Christ in the particular environment in which God has placed him. Further, although the public ministry of the Word is a high office, private witness or personal evangelism has a value which in some respects surpasses even that of preaching, since the message can then be adapted more personally.[4]

Writing about the unique challenge of evangelizing in the 21st century, Ed Stetzer put it directly:

As a follower of Christ, I must live and proclaim that message, or I am not really a follower of Christ. To say, "You can be a Christian as long as you do not share the gospel" is nonsensical. It would be as ridiculous as saying, "Go ahead and be a Muslim, just don't submit to Allah." Or, "Be an observant Jew, but do not follow Torah." Or, "You are free to be a Buddhist so long as you make no effort to follow the eight-fold path." As Charles Spurgeon once said, "Every Christian is either a missionary or an impostor."[5]

Unleashing the Long Tail of Evangelism

Local church always will be the PRIMARY tool for God's will in the world. Other ministries are important but secondary.

Rick Warren

Again, the good news is that we do have a Long Tail to unleash— at least 22 million individual believers who live and work in 22 million relational niches of work, home, family, and relationships. The great news is that activating the Long Tail of evangelism will work. Scripture and history prove it.

The bad news is that there's no simple three-step solution. There's no DVD package that I can sell you, no single seminar that you can attend or speaker you can hire in order to ignite personal evangelism in your people.

The atrophy of the Long Tail, like so many of the problems we face in the national church, goes back to discipleship. Unleashing the Long Tail of evangelism is hard work, because holistic and realistic evangelism training happens best through modeling—to one or a few people at a time.

A lifestyle of evangelism grows out of a mature understanding of life in Christ. Furthermore, a lifestyle of evangelism has to be noticed, imitated, and then implemented. It can't be taught in a classroom or sermon alone. It has to be seen, tasted, and experienced.

This lack of personal evangelism training *as part of holistic discipleship* may track all the way back to senior and CEO-level leaders. Hopefully, in your organization, it does not. For me, one-on-one evangelism has become *more* difficult as I've transitioned from secular journalist to professional pastor. The more God uses me to preach the gospel to large crowds, the easier it is for me to neglect the Spirit's leading in simple conversations along the byways of life. It's almost as if I rationalize away the work of sharing the gospel with one soul because I just shared it with hundreds over the weekend.

That personal struggle for me is, I believe, common for many evangelical leaders. Perhaps we assume the head-based model of the 20th century is God's way of doing things. But in the Scriptures above we've seen that His plan is bigger and broader. As a pastor, I have to intentionally elevate personal evangelism in my life and ministry. Otherwise I get complacent about it.

Recovering personal evangelism—and injecting that into the DNA of the entire Long Tail—is not easy or immediate work. Like physical therapy, it takes time. Here's how we're trying to strengthen the Long Tail in the congregation I serve.

Cornerstone Church (Prescott, Arizona)

You should know I'm not prescribing impossible or theoretical solutions in this book. My ministry is just a few years old, so we are still learning how to apply these biblical principles. But at Cornerstone Church in Prescott, Arizona, we are working to implement these solutions. That includes our intentional efforts to train our people in Spirit-led personal evangelism.

I've been at Cornerstone for about four years. In that time, God has overwhelmingly added to the number of His church. Rapid growth brings many challenges—especially for a ministry that aims to elevate authentic discipleship.

About six months into our rapid growth, we had the funds to hire another pastor. We intentionally hired a pastor of evangelism first—not a worship leader to improve our Sunday gatherings, not an administrator who would tighten all the loose ends, not even a secretary. These were all important needs, but biblically, we chose to elevate evangelism. We needed someone to train us and to lead us by example.

God handpicked an evangelist for us, Pastor Dan Rydberg. Dan leads us as Jesus and Paul led their disciples—by his daily example and unflinching focus. Dan is constantly recruiting disciples and training them—formally and by example—to live like Christ and to share what Christ has done for them. He's constantly training me, too.

Following our choice to hire an evangelism-trainer first, God has continued to exponentially grow and bless our congregation—to the point that within two years we also hired that worship pastor, that executive pastor, that administrative assistant, and other positions, too. God did most of the tenfold growth *after* we put personal evangelism training before glitz or production or anything else.

So how do we unleash the Long Tail at Cornerstone? Well, we don't have a curriculum to sell or a mold to emulate. We've simply made it a top priority to equip God's people as individual evangelists. We've learned it's difficult work—that meaningful evangelism training is not a stand-alone program. It is just another part of holistic disciple-making.

The logistics of training disciples will vary across ministries—along the lines of the discipleship vehicles already in place: home groups, Sunday school classes, missional communities, one-on-one discipleship, and so forth. We can model and train Spirit-led personal evangelism in any of these contexts—if we do it as part of a relational discipleship process.

My point here is not to sell you on one method of modeling or training personal evangelism. My point is to convince you simply to elevate personal evangelism as a priority—first for staff and leaders, and then for every individual disciple in the Long Tail.

Long Tail evangelists aren't Sunday Christians who heard a good pep talk or attended a workshop. Long Tail evangelists are radically transformed disciples who are so passionate about Christ that they don't hesitate to explain Him—to coworkers, to family, and to neighbors. These are the average-Joe Christians we see setting history ablaze with the gospel in the book of Acts.

The apostle Paul wrote this about evangelism: We plant. We water. Only God can bring the increase (1 Corinthians 3:6–7). I believe the same is true of our efforts to revive and resurrect the Long Tail of personal evangelism. We leaders do our part to train our people. And we trust God to do His part. Only He can move 21st-century Americans to be the sort of witnesses we see in Acts.

The question for your ministry is not, How many of your people have you trained? Or, What numbers do you have to show? The question is, Are you planting and watering? Are you discipling your most faithful people in personal evangelism—even when it's tedious and apparently fruitless? And are you trusting God for the increase?

How about the ministry you serve? Is personal evangelism—through each individual in the Long Tail—a high priority? Is it even on the radar? This sort of evangelism isn't as quick and immediate as head-focused, event-based evangelism. It's not as exciting or obvious. But this sort of evangelism, while slower, bears fruit that remains and multiplies.

Imagine how impossible it would be to gather the roughly 294 million non-evangelical Americans to one evangelistic outreach—or even to a series of outreaches. How many hundreds of millions of dollars would such an undertaking cost? Contrast that with the simple reality that if each evangelical believer shares the gospel with ten other Americans, every American who is now alive could hear the gospel directly.

◆ The exponential growth of Christianity started with individual men and women who proclaimed Christ, not only with their lives, but with their words as well. In the United States church we have untapped wells of riches. We have unmined deposits of energy and productivity. We have the potential of 22 million evangelists, each uniquely prepared to invade a "niche" market that no single evangelist could ever enter. And each of these evangelists can work with no need for a salary, benefits, fundraising, nonprofit status, or overhead costs. This is the power of the Long Tail.

I believe in Long Tail evangelism because it's biblical. I also believe in it because I wouldn't know Christ, if not for evangelists from the Long Tail. Chances are, you would not know Christ either, without the Long Tail. Trace your spiritual lineage back far enough and you'll find someone in the Long Tail. The millions who came to Christ through Billy Graham are just one generation removed from a no-name evangelist in the Long Tail—Albert McMakin, the farmhand who kept sharing Christ with Graham and praying for him.

As for me, I met Christ when my dad, a senior pastor, privately explained the gospel to me. My dad met Christ when his dad, a senior pastor, privately explained the gospel to him. My grandpa met Christ in 1936, when an assembly line worker at a Ford motor plant privately explained the gospel to him.

My grandfather did not come to Christ at a massive event. He didn't come to Christ in a church building. He came to Christ in the din and bustle of an industrial factory in Ypsilanti, Michigan. He came to Christ with grease on his hands, as the truth was spoken in love to open ears. Then my grandpa personally led his brothers, sisters, and parents to the Lord. He was able to do so because he was trained by a non-staff disciple. When Earl Peters—a Ford line worker—led my grandpa to Christ, he immediately taught him to read the Bible, share his testimony, and lead others in the sinners' prayer. He also told him he must be part of a Bible-honoring church.

My grandpa spent the next forty-seven years of his life discipling a church congregation that, three generations later, continues making disciples. By modest calculation, well over three thousand legitimate disciples have been made because one person from the long tail—a Mr. Earl Peters—shared the gospel on a Ford production line. I am one of those disciples.

Someone or some ministry taught Earl that he was not exempt from sharing the gospel. Someone taught him that we are all witnesses—that disciples of Christ do that sort of thing. I thank God for that person or ministry. I thank God for Earl Peters. And I thank God for using the spiritual Long Tail.

The Long Tail has always been the muscle behind evangelism. It's time we unleash it again.

Conclusion

The Moment of Decision

In 2004, I walked into a drug house to meet Mickey, a nineteen-year-old heroin addict. Mickey paid rent to her dealer and pimp by selling her body. In exchange, she got foil-wrapped balloons of black tar Mexican heroin—one of the most addictive narcotics in the world.

A source of mine had put me in contact with Mickey so I could profile her for a newspaper piece about heroin. Mickey and I walked to a Jack in the Box, where she shivered and squinted in a booth. We talked about her life. Today, almost ten years later, I can still see the life trapped and struggling behind her icy blue eyes.

Mickey grew up in a well-to-do family. She loved teddy bears as a girl and had hoped to become a lawyer someday. In high school, after fooling around with marijuana and cocaine, she tried heroin. Her first time, she shot up in a bathroom stall at a Barnes & Noble. It was, in her muddled words, "agoshing," an attempt at agonizing. It was the worst drug experience Mickey had ever had. But the next day, she just *had* to have some more. Like most heroin addicts, the opiate enslaved her from that moment on.

Writing Mickey's story was soul-wrenching—seeing the bruised scabs on her neck and learning why she injected there. The arteries on Mickey's arms had frayed to the point that they could no longer take a needle, because she had stabbed so many needles there, so desperately.

Mickey's wounds were tragic. Her history was tragic. Her shriveling body and life were tragic. But the most tragic moment came toward the end of my time with her. In the course of writing the story, I had talked to the best addiction recovery center in the state. They had agreed to take Mickey on—for free. Mickey, who wanted nothing more than to be free from heroin, had a choice to make. She could choose recovery and, like many other addicts, live a normal life. Or she could continue in her slavery—a course that meant sure death.

At her desperate urging, I arranged for Mickey's choice to be as easy as possible. All she had to do was step into a vehicle. All she had to do was agree, and the best help was hers, for free. The day came for Mickey to make her choice. Despite her pleas for help, despite her descriptions of a life in hell, she refused to leave the drug house.

Like Mickey, you and I now stand in a moment of decision. Will we act on what we have learned, or will we settle comfortably back into American church as we have always done it? Will we strain to lead Christ's church closer to His plan, or will we be content to pay our mortgages, count our attendances, and lead comfortable American lives? Our choice, like Mickey's, will have lifelong and eternal consequences.

We stand at the hinge of a great moving in Christ's church. God, in His plan, placed us at this time of historic opportunity. His most valuable possession—His bride—is ours to guide gently and boldly through the 21st century. She will either draw closer to His heart and plan, or drift further from it. Her spiritual decay or restoration depends, in your sphere, on you and your leadership.

We do not know every solution to the church's many problems. What we do know is this: The United States church is moving with speed and momentum in a direction that includes lethargic discipleship, sputtering evangelism, abandoned unity, pending bankruptcy, and failed ambassadorship to the lost. We are in need of a historic course correction, lest we run aground.

It is not the first time that Christ's bride has needed such a redirection. And we are not the first leaders to sense almighty God orchestrating such a massive turning of His church, in our hearts.

Around 1360, a professor of theology looked at the church in his day. He compared that church to God's Word. And he reported: Here's where we're off. Here are the areas where we've veered away from the New Testament and from Jesus Christ.

That professor didn't have great influence, at first. He didn't have a plan or a "solution" for every problem. He simply invested in disciples—training each one to teach a pure gospel, to depend on Scripture alone, and to be reproductive in making disciples.

John Wycliffe didn't know his life would change world history. He didn't know, nor could he have imagined, that his simple faithfulness would lay the kindling to ignite the Protestant Reformation. Wycliffe didn't know that, by simply being true to God's Word, he would change the history of nations, of the world, of the church, and of Christ's kingdom.

Wycliffe, Zwingli, Luther, and Calvin all compared the church of their day to the church described in God's Word. They were not perfect, but they were faithful in saying, Here's where we've veered from God's plan.

If we could import the Reformers here, to the 21st century, they would surely be doing the same—not as distant critics but as self-sacrificing laborers. When we offer our fortunes, our health, and our hearts to discover and implement Christ's way for His church, we stand in rank with the Reformers.

We stand in rank, too, with the great evangelical leaders of the 20th century: Billy Graham, Harold Ockenga, and Carl F. H. Henry. These were young men who, in the 1940s and '50s, parsed a difficult trail between theological liberalism on the left and belligerent reactionism on the right. Their guide was not culture or feedback. Their guide was God's Word. Like the Reformers, they never could have imagined the global and eternal impact of their simple faithfulness to Christ and His Word.

Now, you and I find ourselves in a similar moment of church history. We stand—as Graham, Wycliffe, and Luther—in a time of confusing cultural change, a time when Christ's church can drift further into impotence or step tenaciously toward kingdom power. The future of evangelicalism lies, as always, in the resolve and choices of we who will lead in the next decades.

It is up to us to guide ministries, families, and souls through
the challenges of today. It's up to us to keep Christ, His gospel,
and His Word our craving. My prayer is that God uses this book
as a practical tool—to help you understand and lead your corner
of the kingdom closer to the heart of the King.

We have seen many biblical solutions. A common theme ties
many of them together. More than anything else, 21st-Century
Evangelicalism depends on making disciples—who then make
disciples (2 Timothy 2:2). It requires a values exchange that trades
macro for micro, numbers for individuals, production for transformation—in our microchurches as well as our megachurches. This
values exchange will—in time—make ministries much larger, as
well as much deeper. Spiritually, it will give staying power. I believe
this values exchange can be done biblically and powerfully within
any number of American church models—from purpose-driven
churches to Reformed churches, to missional, community-based,
and denominational churches.

Authentic discipleship will incarnate in highly individual ways.
But the priority itself must become broadly universal in order for
evangelicalism to recover its spiritual vibrancy. Elevating individual
discipleship is a paradox—much like dying to self to find life.
When it comes to sustained numeric growth across generations,
institutional stability, financial viability, and cultural influence,
our best insurance is not deep pockets or corporate planning but
individual disciple-making.

If we will commit ourselves to training disciples who then train
more disciples, we can reverse each of the 21st-century declines
documented in this book. Such reproductive disciple-making roots
young believers (Bleeding/Healing). It equips them to evangelize
and make disciples of their own (Sputtering/Re-igniting), and it
showcases what it looks like to be proactively GOOD in a hostile
culture (Hated/Good). Relational discipleship models how we
elevate the gospel above our disagreements with other evangelicals
(Dividing/Uniting). Real-life discipleship also teaches death to self
in every area of life, including finances (Bankrupt/Solvent).

The Reformers before us abandoned comfort and convenience
to boldly lead Christ's church. If we wish to lead His church

now, we must abandon many comforts from the 20th-century church paradigm.

Just as Wycliffe and Luther didn't know all the solutions to the troubled church of their day, we may not know today exactly *how* to apply every one of these solutions in our own ministries. But know this: If we will abandon 20th-century priorities in order to pursue Christ's priorities, He will provide the wisdom and means to make disciples. If we will remain committed to leading Christ's church *His* way, He will mature His bride—one most valuable possession at a time.

The Reformers were far from perfect. We don't need to be perfect, either. But the Reformers were faithful. Despite physical, spiritual, emotional, and financial setbacks, they never gave up. Now it's up to you and me to lead in the same manner. Despite criticism from other Christians, the best Reformers abandoned the traditions of church to rediscover the discipleship of Christ and the sola of Scriptura.

You may not believe that God could use you as He did Graham or Wycliffe. He can. Together with me, renew your commitment to Christ, to His Word, and to His way of making disciples. We will together lead 21st-Century Evangelicalism to be a more authentic, nimble, faithful, and God-glorifying church.

It will not be easy.

But it will be worth it.

This is our moment of decision.

-=≈=-

Connect with the author, find free resources, and sign up for up dates about the United States church at JohnSDickerson.com

On Twitter: JohnSDickerson

On Facebook: facebook.com/JohnSDickerson

Appendixes

Appendix A

"Is the Author's Church Declining? Maybe That's Why He's Pessimistic"

Some will suspect that if I believe the national church is declining, I must pastor a declining church. By God's grace, I do not.

I grew up in a thriving congregation, led by my grandfather, and, for the last twenty-five years, led by my dad. After college I served at an Arizona megachurch with attendance of about 6,500. That congregation also continues to thrive.

I now serve as senior pastor of Cornerstone in Prescott, Arizona. In my time there, God has grown our number from about fifty to more than five hundred regular attendees. That's tenfold growth in four years, in a small city. God has blessed Cornerstone with growth in depth, discipleship, and conversions, as well as rapid growth in size. We praise Him for that.

Like most evangelicals these days, I attend one of the fastest-growing churches in town. The conclusions in this book are based on national research, not on personal experience.

Appendix B

"Aren't There Positive Things Happening in Evangelicalism, Too?"

Answer: Yes, there are dozens of positive trends in United States evangelicalism. Our movement is rich with leaders and congregations who are rediscovering and revolutionizing biblical Christianity. You probably know some of these pastors and churches. Many cities have at least one church that is an exception to some of these national trends. I get to serve one of those churches. Unfortunately, as of now, these churches are just that—exceptions.

Also, as noted in the Inflated chapter, many of these rapidly growing churches are simply attracting transfer believers from other churches. This has been the case with my own congregation. Exciting as Cornerstone's rapid growth has been, it has also demonstrated that growing churches in the United States are often attracting more transfer sheep than new believers—even if that is not their goal. Our aim at Cornerstone has never been to attract existing believers from other congregations, and yet only a small percentage of our new folks each month are brand-new believers. This is common with rapidly growing churches.

Appendix C

Defining "Evangelical"

Evangelicalism is a broad and motley movement. Our most respected observers have yet to reach consensus on exactly who evangelicals are and where we are headed. This book is primarily a practical tool, not an academic one. As such, we have to settle on some practical definition. We will consider three important definitions of "evangelical" for this work.

First, British theologian and professor Dr. Alister McGrath writes, "Evangelical is thus the term chosen by evangelicals to refer to themselves, as representing most adequately the central concern of the movement for the safeguarding and articulation of the evangel—the good news of God which has been made known and made possible in Jesus Christ."[1]

This theological definition is of interest because our study is not concerned with those who are evangelical only in culture, while not personally being able to articulate the gospel. That's a strict definition by a sociologist's measure, but I would argue that it is not a strict definition by Christ's measure—or by the measure of the New Testament.

Like McGrath, I narrow my definition of evangelical to those who are familiar enough with the Evangel to articulate it to some degree.

The next definition we will consider is the Bebbington quadrilateral, an increasingly common benchmark for academics and sociologists.[2] David Bebbington points to four values, convictions, or attitudes. When an individual holds all four of these, he or she is definitively evangelical, Bebbington says. The quadrilateral includes

1. Biblicism, a particular regard for the Bible (e.g., all spiritual truth is to be found in its pages)
2. Crucicentrism, a focus on the atoning work of Christ on the cross
3. Conversionism, the belief that human beings need to be converted
4. Activism, the belief that the gospel needs to be expressed in effort.[3]

Bebbington's definition is, in some ways, more restrictive than McGrath's and in other ways less. It only requires a focus on the cross and conversion, rather than an ability to articulate it. However, it also requires activism and biblicism, which McGrath's definition does not. Biblicism and some degree of activism are clearly values of mainstream evangelicalism, so I include them in my definition.

The third definition to consider is Francis Schaeffer's.[4] He wrote in *The Great Evangelical Disaster* that to be evangelical is to be "Bible-believing without shutting one's self off from the full spectrum of life, and in trying to bring Christianity into effective contact with the current needs of society, government and culture. It had a connotation of leading people to Christ as Savior, but then trying to be salt and light in the culture."

Schaeffer emphasizes the "full-spectrum" of living in the culture. Here, Schaeffer points out the practical distinctive of American evangelicals. We have a heritage of intentionally interacting with the culture in a positive way, rather than isolating and reacting or submitting and capitulating to it. This "engaged orthodoxy"[5] stands noticeably apart from the spiritual bunker mentality that defined American fundamentalism. It also stands apart from the spongy plurality that defines theologically liberal Protestants. Billy

Graham, Harold Ockenga, and Carl F. H. Henry intentionally cut a path between both extremes when they birthed neo-evangelicalism in the 1940s and '50s. Thus, United States evangelicalism toes this practical footing between two extreme responses to a changing society.

With those definitions considered, we should note that the "movement" of evangelicalism is exactly that—a thrust or direction of millions who disagree about everything except Christ as Savior and the Bible as God's Word. Evangelicalism is not static.

I sometimes picture United States evangelicalism as a massive iceberg floating in the Atlantic. Gigantic icebergs fizzle and pop as their edges melt. Sometimes stretching for miles or city blocks, such bergs can split or flip without warning. Some sections—maybe the size of an apartment building—may be covered in soil and rocks, from the land where the berg slid off into the ocean. Other parts of the iceberg are bone-white. Still other areas stream with the crystal blue of freshwater ice melt. At any time, car-sized chunks may fall off of the berg, without warning.

United States evangelicalism—a singular floating and shrinking berg—has countless unique features and contradictory edges. I am setting out in this project to measure the trajectory of the berg itself, the course of the entire beast. I am not setting out to measure every detail. As such, many developments on the edges of the larger organism—important as they are—cannot be included in this book.

Our work here is not to predict the future, but to identify the existing and undeniable trajectory of the movement. In essence, this book concludes that these trends are the present trajectory of the entire movement. Thus, *barring a radical change of course*, they are the direction of our near future.

Inherent in any work of this nature is the risk of oversimplification. To identify the most influential trends in a movement of millions is daunting, let alone to do so in a movement as diverse, disorganized, and intangible as United States evangelicalism.

People who have spent their lives studying the breadth and impact of evangelicalism still disagree about the movement's actual size, boundaries, and recent direction. As Christian Smith notes,

"Many observers, including both academic sociologists . . . and respected evangelical leaders . . . view evangelicalism as either floundering in its mission or actually disintegrating under the pressures of the modern world around it. Others . . . take a more benign view, predicting bright prospects."[6]

Notes

Introduction

1. George Friedman, *The Next 100 Years* (New York: Anchor Books, 2010), 3.
2. Nouriel Roubini, "Eight Who Saw the Crisis Coming," *Fortune*, August 2008, http://money.cnn.com/galleries/2008/fortune/0808/gallery.whosawitcoming.fortune/2.html.
3. Stephen Mihm, "Dr. Doom," *New York Times Magazine*, August 15, 2008, http://www.nytimes.com/2008/08/17/magazine/17pessimist-t.html.
4. Tom Sine, "A Wakeup Call for Evangelicals," Patheos.com, August 13, 2010, http://www.patheos.com/Resources/Additional-Resources/A-Wakeup-Call-for-Evangelicals.html.
5. Marcus Buckingham and Donald O. Clifton, *Now, Discover Your Strengths* (New York: The Free Press, 2001), 115.
6. Ibid.
7. George Barna, *Futurecast* (Carol Stream, IL: BarnaBooks, 2011), 198.
8. Gabe Lyons, *The Next Christians* (New York: Doubleday Religion, 2010), 11.
9. Gregory P. Elder, Bible.org, http://bible.org/illustration/sand-castles.

Chapter 1: Inflated

1. Ryan Avent, "The Great Recession," *Economist*, January 8, 2011, http://www.economist.com/blogs/freeexchange/2011/01/great_recession. Avent writes, "Most attendees" at the American Economic Association conference in Denver, January 8, 2011, consider "rising home prices" as a trigger in the Great Recession.
2. John N. Vaughan, "Go Figure," *Christianity Today*, May 27, 2011, http://johnnvaughan.wordpress.com/2010/12/13/the-2010-americas-100-largest-churches-list-is-published/.
3. Scott Thumma and Warren Bird, "National Survey of Megachurch Attendees," Hartford Institute for Religion and Research, 1: "Many attenders come from other churches, but nearly a quarter haven't been in any church for a long time before coming to a megachurch." Conversely, 75 percent do come from other churches.

4. Michael Hyatt, http://michaelhyatt.com/why-imprints-don't-matter.html.

5. United States Census Bureau calculation that the United States Population is 316 million in 2012. http://www.census.gov/population/www/projections/summary tables.html.

6. Adelle M. Banks, "Poll: Evangelicals See Declining Influence in United States," *Christianity Today Live Blog*, June 23, 2011, http://blog.christianitytoday.com/ctliveblog/archives/2011/06/poll_evangelica.html.

7. M. Alex Johnson, "Southern Baptists End 8 Year Disney Boycott," msnbc.com, June 22, 2005, http://www.msnbc.msn.com/id/8318263/ns/us_news/t/southern-baptists-end-year-disney-boycott/.

8. Christine Wicker, *The Fall of the Evangelical Nation* (New York: Harper One, 2008), 67.

9. Thom Rainer and Sam Rainer, *Essential Church? Reclaiming a Generation of Dropouts* (Nashville: B & H Books, 2008), 8.

10. Barry Kosmin and Ariela Keysar, "2009 American Religious Identification Survey, Summary," (Trinity College, 2009).

11. Chip Berlet, "Religion and Politics in the United States: Nuances You Should Know," *The Public Eye Magazine*, Summer 2003, http://www.publiceye.org/magazine/v17n2/evangelical-demographics.html.

12. George Barna, *Futurecast* (Carol Stream, IL: BarnaBooks, 2011), 127.

13. Christian Smith, *American Evangelicalism, Embattled and Thriving* (Chicago: The University of Chicago Press, 1998), 1, 221–222.

14. David T. Olson, *The American Church in Crisis* (Grand Rapids, MI: Zondervan, 2008), 16.

15. Ibid.

16. George Barna, "Survey Explores Who Qualifies As an Evangelical," *The Barna Update*, January 18, 2007, http://www.barna.org/barna-update/article/13-culture/111-survey-explores-who-qualifies-as-an-evangelical.

17. Wicker, *The Fall of the Evangelical Nation*, 19, 21.

18. Bob Smietana, "Nation's Largest Protestant Group Faces Decline," *USA Today*, June 11, 2011, http://www.usatoday.com/news/religion/2011-06-12-baptisms_11_ST_N.htm.

19. Wicker, *The Fall of the Evangelical Nation*, 24–25.

20. United States Census Bureau, United States Population Clock, http://www.census.gov/main/www/popclock.html.

21. Haya El Nasser, "How Will the USA Cope With Unprecedented Growth?" *USA Today*, October 26, 2006, http://www.usatoday.com/news/nation/2006-10-26-100-million_x.htm.

22. Applying the percentage of Muslims in Egypt to the population of the greater Cairo region, there are about 18 million Muslims in the "city of a thousand minarets."

Chapter 2: Hated

1. Ephesians 6:11 describes the devil as one who schemes. First Peter 5:8 further demonstrates this.

2. Crystal Dixon, "Gay Right and Wrongs: Another Perspective," *Toledo Free Press*, April 18, 2008, http://www.toledofreepress.com/2008/04/18/gay-rights-and -wrongs-another-perspective/.

3. Gail Burkhardt, "Crystal Dixon Sues UT for Rights Violations," *Toledo Free Press*, December 5, 2008, http://www.toledofreepress.com/2008/12/05/crystal -dixon-sues-ut-for-rights-violations/.

4. Sohail Inayatullah, ed., "The Views of Futurists," *The Knowledge Base of Futures Studies*, Vol. 4 (Brisbane: Foresight International, 2001).

5. George Barna, *Futurecast* (Carol Stream, IL: BarnaBooks, 2011), x.

6. Gautam Malkani, "Britain Burns the Colour of 'A Clockwork Orange,'" *Financial Times*, August 12, 2011, http://www.ft.com/intl/cms/s/0/8c42acba-c40f-11e0 -b302-00144feabdc0.html.

7. Ray Kurzweil, "The Law of Accelerating Returns," Kurzweil Accelerating Intelligence, March 7, 2001, http://www.kurzweilai.net/the-law-of-accelerating-returns.

8. Ibid.

9. David Jeremiah, *I Never Thought I'd See the Day!* (New York: FaithWords, 2011), Table of Contents.

10. Ibid., 152.

11. Francis A. Shaeffer, *The Great Evangelical Disaster* (Wheaton, IL: Crossway Books, 1984), 23. Used by permission of Crossway, a publishing ministry of Good News Publishers, Wheaton, IL 60187, www.crossway.org.

12. Ibid., 29.

13. Barna, *Futurecast*, 125.

14. Ross Douthat, "Crises of Faith," *Atlantic Monthly*, July, 2007, http://www .theatlantic.com/magazine/archive/2007/07/crises-of-faith/5967/2/.

15. Ross Douthat, *Bad Religion* (New York: Free Press, 2012), 142.

16. Ross Douthat, "Crises of Faith."

17. Matt Branaugh, "Google Cuts Churches Out of Non-Profit Program, *Christianity Today*, August 25, 2011, http://www.christianitytoday.com/ct/2011/august web-only/googlecutschurchesout.html.

18. Peter Wood, *Chronicle of Higher Education*, April 6, 2011, http://chronicle .com/blogs/innovations/preferred-colleagues/29160.

19. Peter Wood, *Chronicle of Higher Education*, December 10, 2010, http://chronicle .com/blogs/innovations/potentially-evangelical/28135.

20. Alan Cooperman, "Is There Disdain for Evangelicals in the Classroom?" *Washington Post*, May 5, 2007, http://www.washingtonpost.com/wp-dyn/content/article /2007/05/04/AR2007050401990.html.

21. "Missouri School Sued by Student Who Refused to Support Gay Adoptions," *USA Today*, November 2, 2006, http://www.usatoday.com/news/nation/2006-11-02 -gay-adoption_x.htm.

22. Ed Stetzer, "Willow Creek, Homosexuality, and the Future of Evangelical Response," *The Lifeway Research Blog*, August 11, 2011, http://www.edstetzer.com /2011/08/willowcreek-homosexuality-and.html.

23. Claire Courchane, "Young Americans Likely to Back Gay Marriage," *Washington Times*, June 9, 2011, http://www.washingtontimes.com/news/2011/jun/9/young -americans-likely-to-back-gay-marriage/.

24. Frank Newport, The Gallup Poll, May 20, 2011, http://www.gallup.com/poll/147662/first-time-majority-americans-favor-legal-gay-marriage.aspx. Survey results and graphic used by permission.

25. David Kinnaman and Gabe Lyons, *UnChristian* (Grand Rapids, MI: Baker, 2007), 92, 93.

26. Ibid., 92.

27. Christian Huygen, "Lesbian, Gay, Bisexual, Transgender People With Mental Illness: Mental Health Concerns of LGBT Consumers," Medscape General Medicine, http://www.medscape.com/viewarticle/529619_3.

28. Alix Spiegel, "81 Words," *This American Life*, originally aired January 18, 2002, http://www.thisamericanlife.org/radio-archives/episode/204/81-words.

29. Sheryl Gay Stolberg, "Christian Counseling by Hopeful's Spouse Prompts Questions," *New York Times*, July 16, 2011, http://www.nytimes.com/2011/07/17/us/politics/17clinic.html. "A 2007 task force put together by the American Psychological Association concluded that 'efforts to change sexual orientation are unlikely to be successful and involve some risk of harm.'"

30. Mary Guindon, Alan Green, and Fred Hanna, "Intolerance and Psychopathology: Toward a General Diagnosis for Racism, Sexism, and Homophobia," *American Journal of Orthopsychiatry*, Vol. 73 (April 2003): 167–76.

31. Wiley Online Library, March 24, 2010, http://onlinelibrary.wiley.com/doi/10.1037/0002-9432.73.2.167/abstract.

32. European Parliament resolution on homophobia in Europe, P6_TA-PROV(2006)0018, Homophobia in Europe, PE 368.248. Available at: http://ilga-europe.org/home/news/latest_news/ilga_europe_welcomes_europarliament_s_resolution_on_homophobia_in_europe.

33. Ibid.

34. For more information on this California law, see http://www.huffingtonpost.com/2012/09/30/jerry-brown-sb-1172-gay-conversion-therapy-california_n_1926855.html and http://leginfo.legislature.ca.gov/faces/billNavClient.xhtml?bill_id=201120120SB1172.

35. Stetzer, "Willow Creek, Homosexuality, and the Future of Evangelical Response."

36. Stolberg, "Christian Counseling by Hopeful's Spouse Prompts Questions."

37. Brian Bond, The White House, June 29, 2011, http://www.whitehouse.gov/blog/2011/06/29/lgbt-pride-month-white-house.

38. Ed Stetzer, "The Pornification of the American Culture," *The Lifeway Research Blog*, July 27, 2011, http://www.edstetzer.com/2011/07/the-pornification-of-american.html.

39. *Journal of Urban Health: Bulletin of New York Academy of Medicine* article, reported by Jeanette Torres, ABC News Radio, December 20, 2011, http://abcnewsradioonline.com/health-news/teens-as-young-as-14-engaging-in-group-sex-study-finds.html.

40. Ibid.

41. Susan Donaldson James, "Philadelphia Gives Condoms to 11-Year-Olds," *ABC News*, April 17, 2011, http://abcnews.go.com/Health/philadelphia-kids-young-11-condoms-nations-highest-teen/story?id=13373272#.

42. Nancy Dillon, "$23M Bail for LA Teacher Accused of Feeding Semen to Kids," *New York Daily News*, February 1, 2012, http://articles.nydailynews.com/2012-02-01/news/31015005_1_miramonte-elementary-school-cops-spoon.

Chapter 3: Dividing

1. Woodland Hills, http://whchurch.org/sermons-media/sermons/sermons-2000-2005/2004-sermons.

2. Laurie Goodstein, "Disowning Conservative Politics, Evangelical Pastor Rattles Flock," *The New York Times*, July 30, 2006, http://www.nytimes.com/2006/07/30/us/30pastor.html.

3. Ibid.

4. Michael Luo, "Evangelicals Debate the Meaning of 'Evangelical,'" *New York Times*, April 16, 2006, http://www.nytimes.com/2006/04/16/weekinreview/16luo.html.

5. Kinnaman and Lyons, *UnChristian* (Grand Rapids, MI: Baker, 2007), 154.

6. John C. Green, "The American Religious Landscape and Political Attitudes: A Baseline for 2004," 3, https://www.uakron.edu/pages/bliss/docs/Religious_Landscape_2004.pdf.

7. Frank Newport and Joseph Carroll, "Another Look at Evangelicals in America Today," Gallup News Service, December 2, 2005, http://www.gallup.com/poll/20242/another-look-evangelicals-america-today.aspx.

8. D. Michael Lindsay, *Faith in the Halls of Power* (Oxford: Oxford University Press, 2007), 28.

9. Karl Giberson and Randall Stephens, "The Evangelical Rejection of Reason," *New York Times*, October 17, 2011, http://www.nytimes.com/2011/10/18/opinion/the-evangelical-rejection-of-reason.html.

10. Jon Meacham, "The End of Christian America," *Newsweek*, April 3, 2009, http://www.newsweek.com/2009/04/03/the-end-of-christian-america.html.

11. Laurie Goodstein, "Obama Wins Unlikely Allies in Immigration," *New York Times*, July 18, 2010, http://www.nytimes.com/2010/07/19/us/politics/19evangelicals.html.

12. John MacArthur, *Why Government Can't Save You* (Grand Rapids, MI: Zondervan, 2000), ix.

13. Ibid., 8.

14. Venessa Mendenhall, "Are Young Evangelicals Leaning Left?" *PBS*, November 21, 2006, http://www.pbs.org/newshour/generation-next/demographic/religion3_11-21.html.

15. Dan Cox, "Young White Evangelicals: Less Republican, Still Conservative," The Pew Forum, September 28, 2007, http://pewforum.org/Politics-and-Elections/Young-White-Evangelicals-Less-Republican-Still-Conservative.aspx.

16. Ibid.

17. Randall Balmer's endorsement for Elisa Harris's *Raised Right* (Colorado Springs: WaterBrook Press, 2011), i.

18. Jim Wallis, a contributed essay, "Not Left or Right—Deeper," in the book *unChristian*, 174.

19. Mark Noll, Nathan Hatch, and George Marsden, from *The Search for Christian America* (Colorado Springs: Helmers & Howard, 1989), quoted by Jon Meacham,

"The End of Christian America," *Newsweek*, April 3, 2009, http://www.thedailybeast
.com/newsweek/2009/04/03/the-end-of-christian-america.html.

20. Ibid.

21. Goodstein, "Obama Wins Unlikely Allies in Immigration."

22. Rob Kerby, "Is Hispanic Growth Strengthening Our Churches?" Beliefnet, April
1, 2011, http://blog.beliefnet.com/on_the_front_lines_of_the_culture_wars/2011/04
/hispanic-growth-said-to-be-strengthening-u-s-churches.html.

23. Soong-Chan Rah, "The End of Christianity in America?" *Patheos*, August 6,
2010, http://www.patheos.com/Resources/Additional-Resources/End-of-Christianity
-in-America.html.

24. Lisa Miller, "How Sarah Palin Is Reshaping the Religious Right," *Newsweek*,
June 11, 2010, http://www.newsweek.com/2010/06/11/saint-sarah.html.

25. D. A. Carson, The Gospel Coalition, "Generational Conflict in Ministry,"
originally published in *Themelios* 36, no. 2 (August 2011), http://thegospelcoalition
.org/themelios/article/generational_conflict_in_ministry.

26. Luo, "Evangelicals Debate the Meaning of 'Evangelical.'"

Chapter 4: Bankrupt

1. Mark Martin, Calvary Community Church, sermon illustration.

2. Unless some other factor changes radically.

3. Amy Taxin, AP wire story, *Huffington Post*, October 18, 2010, http://www
.huffingtonpost.com/2010/10/18/crystal-cathedral-bankrup_n_767219.html.

4. Deepa Bharath, "Crystal Cathedral Founder Asks for Help," *Orange County
Register*, October 24, 2010, http://www.ocregister.com/news/church-272623-schuller
-father.html.

5. "Regent U. Struggles to Stay Afloat (Updated), Court Rules that Feeding Poor
Is Not Religious, and Other News," *Christianity Today*, September 2, 2010, http://
www.christianitytoday.com/ct/2010/september/7.14.html.

6. Cal Thomas, "Closing One Door, Opening Another," syndicated column, June
7, 2007, http://www.calthomas.com/index.php?news=237.

7. The actual number is larger but unknown. This figure represents only the annual
evangelical revenues tracked by the Evangelical Council for Financial Accountability
(ECFA).

8. Larry Eskridge and Mark A. Noll, eds., *More Money, More Ministry: Money
and Evangelicals in Recent North American History* (Grand Rapids, MI: Eerdmans,
2000), Joel A. Carpenter chapter.

9. Mark Noll, *A History of Christianity in the United States and Canada* (Grand
Rapids, MI: Eerdmans, 1992), 179, 181–187, 532–537.

10. Of course, this divide is also in our Catholic and even Protestant roots and it can,
to a degree, be soundly argued biblically from the New Testament missionary journeys.

11. George Barna, *Futurecast* (Carol Stream, IL: BarnaBooks, 2011), 191.

12. The CIA World Factbook documents Iceland's gross domestic product at $12.57
billion: https://www.cia.gov/library/publications/the-world-factbook/geos/ic.html.

13. Ronald Sider, "The Scandal of the Evangelical Conscience," *Books and Culture*, January 1, 2005. Quoted at http://library.generousgiving.org/page.asp?sec=4&page=161#53.

14. George Barna, *Revolution* (Carol Stream, IL: BarnaBooks, 2005), 33.

15. George Barna, "Tithing Down 62% in the Past Year," Barna Research Group, May 19, 2003, http://www.barna.org/barna-update/article/5-barna-update/121-tithing -down-62-in-the-past-year?q=giving.

16. John L. Ronsvalle and Sylvia Ronsvalle, *The State of Church Giving through 2004: Will We Will?* (Champaign, IL: empty tomb, inc., 2006), http://library.generous giving.org/page.asp?sec=50&page=609#RonsvalleJS3.

17. Barna Group, "Americans Donate Billions to Charity, But Giving to Churches Has Declined," April 25, 2005, http://www.barna.org/barna-update/article/5-barna-update/180-americans-donate-billions-to-charity-but-giving-to-churches-has-declined ?q=giving.

18. Brian Kluth, "Twenty Mega-Trends Impacting Christian Fund Raising," Kingdom Seekers, n.d. Quoted at http://library.generousgiving.org/page.asp?sec =28&page=279.

19. Biblical Stewardship, http://biblicalstewardship.net/statistical-research-on-stewardship/; "Eighty percent of the world's evangelical wealth is in North America," citing *Generous Living* (Grand Rapids, MI: Zondervan, 1997), 201, and Larry Eskridge, *Defining Evangelicalism* (Wheaton, IL: Institute for the Study of American Evangelicals, n.d.).

20. John L. and Sylvia Ronsvalle, *The State of Church Giving Through 2009*, 21st ed. (Champaign, IL: empty tomb, inc., 2011), 104–105. Used by permission. See also footnote #3 in chapter 10.

21. The Pew Forum on Religion and Public Life, "United States Religious Landscape Survey," February 2008, 81–82.

22. Center for Disease Control, "Number of Deaths and Death Rates, by Age, Race, and Sex: United States, 2006," http://www.disastercenter.com/cdc/Table_3_2006.html.

23. Blackbaud's Target Analytics Nonprofit Cooperative Database. Used by permission. See also "Young Donors and Other Mythical Creatures," May 2010, *Fund Raising Success*.

24. Samuel Freedman, "Congregations Reeling from Decline in Donations," *New York Times*, September 25, 2010, A19, http://www.nytimes.com/2010/09/25/us/25 religion.html.

25. Barna Group, "Donors Reduce Giving, Brace for the Long Haul," February 8, 2010, http://www.barna.org/barna-update/article/18-congregations/341-the-economys -impact-part-3-of-3 donors-reduce-giving-brace-for-the-long-haul?q=giving.

26. Freedman, paraphrasing Charles E. Zech, "Congregations Reeling from Decline in Donations."

27. George Barna, "Churches Lose Financial Ground in 2000," Barna Research Group, June 5, 2001, http://www.barna.org/barna-update/article/5-barna-update /51-churches-lose-financial-ground-in-2000.

28. Kluth, "Twenty Mega-Trends Impacting Christian Fund Raising." See also http://www.kluth.org/fundraising/20MegaTrends.htm.

29. Freedman, "Congregations Reeling from Decline in Donations."

30. Tamara Audi, "Crystal Cathedral's Cracks Show in Bankruptcy Filing," *Wall Street Journal*, October, 23, 2010, http://online.wsj.com/article/SB100014240527023040 11604575565060738315760.html.

Chapter 5: Bleeding

1. Josh McDowell, *The Last Christian Generation* (Holiday, FL: Green Key Books, 2006), 13.

2. Cathy Lynn Grossman, "Young Adults Aren't Sticking With Church," *USA Today*, August 6, 2007, http://www.usatoday.com/news/religion/2007-08-06-church -dropouts_N.htm.

3. Cathy Lynn Grossman, "Survey: 72% of Millennials 'More Spiritual Than Religious,'" *USA Today*, April 27, 2010, http://www.usatoday.com/news/religion/2010 -04-27-1Amillfaith27_ST_N.htm.

4. Drew Dyck, *Generation Ex-Christian* (Chicago: Moody, 2010), 17.

5. Ed Stetzer, *Lost and Found* (Nashville: B & H, 2009), 1.

6. Scott McConnellon, "LifeWay Research Finds Reasons 18- to 22-Year-Olds Drop Out of Church," August 07, 2007, http://www.lifeway.com/Article/LifeWay -Research-finds-reasons-18-to-22-year-olds-drop-out-of-church.

7. David Kinnaman, *You Lost Me* (Grand Rapids, MI: Baker, 2011), 12–13.

8. Rodney Stark and Byron Johnson, "Religion and the Bad News Bearers," *Wall Street Journal*, August 26, 2011, http://online.wsj.com/article/SB100014240531119034 80904576510692691734916.html.

9. McConnellon, "LifeWay Research Finds Reasons 18- to 22-Year-Olds Drop Out of Church."

10. No study can predict the future behavior of these prodigals over the next decades. The LifeWay study does not purport to predict the future behavior of these former church attendees. We will not know with certainty if those young people may return in twenty or thirty years until twenty or thirty years from now.

11. Dyck, *Generation Ex-Christian*, 188.

12. Christian Smith and Patricia Snell, *Souls in Transition* (Oxford: Oxford University Press, 2009), 252.

13. Ibid., 254.

14. Dyck, *Generation Ex-Christian*, 192.

15. During a two-hour phone interview conducted on May 7, 2010.

16. These conclusions were reached by combining multiple reports.

To conclude that there are about 3.7 million United States evangelicals ages 18–29, the two following reports were combined. This age group accounts for 17 percent of the evangelical church, according to the Pew Forum on Religion and Public Life, "United States Religious Landscape Survey," February 2008, 81–82. In chapter 1 (Inflated), I cited four researchers who estimate the size of United States Evangelicalism to be about 22 million. Seventeen percent of 22 million is 3.74 million. How many from that generation will depart? Josh McDowell, LifeWay, and the Barna Group have all found that about 70 percent leave the church. Seventy percent of the 3.7 million in this group comes out to about 2.6 million. Obviously, the rate of departure is not evenly distributed across each year and day. However, if it were, then 260,000 would leave during each of the 10 years between ages 18 and 29. Again, if this were evenly distributed, it would mean that 712 evangelicals ages 18 to 29 walk away each day. How many return? LifeWay has found that 35 percent who leave eventually return (see footnote above in this same chapter). Thirty-five percent of 2.6 million is about 900,000 who will return. The balance is about 1.7 million who may not return. The

Big Picture: After 10 years, the 18- to 29-year-olds will be ages 28–39. There will be a new group of 18- to 29-year-olds. Present generational trends indicate that the rate of departure is not slowing but accelerating. If two generations in a row exit at this rate, then about 5.2 million will have left the church within 20 years. Roughly 3.4 million of them may never return.

17. Christian Smith and Melinda Lundquist Denton, *Soul Searching* (Oxford: Oxford University Press, 2005), 162–70.

18. Ibid., 262.

19. Kinnaman, *You Lost Me*, 115.

20. Tom Sine, "A Wakeup Call for Evangelicals," Patheos.com, August 13, 2010, http://www.patheos.com/Resources/Additional-Resources/A-Wakeup-Call-for-Evangelicals.html.

21. George Barna, "Barna Survey Examines Changes in Worldview Among Christians Over the Past 13 Years," Barna Group, March 6, 2009, http://www.barna.org/barna-update/article/21-transformation/252-barna-survey-examines-changes-in-worldview-among-christians-over-the-past-13-years.

22. George Barna, *Revolution* (Carol Stream, IL: BarnaBooks, 2005), 35.

23. Julia Duin, *Quitting Church* (Grand Rapids, MI: Baker, 2008), 23.

24. Quoted by Kenda Creasy Dean, *Almost Christian: What the Faith of Our Teenagers Is Telling the American Church* (Oxford: Oxford University Press, 2010), 25.

25. Kinnaman, *You Lost Me*, 21.

26. Barna, *Revolution*, 31.

Chapter 6: Sputtering

1. Of course, Christ gave hundreds of other commands, but they all serve this one command and ultimately serve to glorify God by gathering and redeeming worshipers for Him, until Christ returns.

2. See John 15:15–17: ". . . go and bear fruit—fruit that will last."

3. Mark Noll, *A History of Christianity in the United States and Canada* (Grand Rapids, MI: Eerdmans, 1992), 476. Gallup's self-reported "born again" figure has dropped from 49 percent in 1958 to 41 percent in 2008. Gallup and company have been asking Americans this question since the 1940s, giving us a clear benchmark of those who consider themselves born again. While I have critically suggested that not all self-claiming "born agains" are evangelicals, the group certainly includes evangelicals. This is the only national survey with such a lengthy history.

4. George Barna, *Futurecast* (Carol Stream, IL: BarnaBooks, 2011), 205.

5. Barry Kosmin and Ariela Keysar, "2009 American Religious Identification Survey, Summary" (Hartford, CT: Trinity College, 2009), 17.

6. Julia Duin, *Quitting Church* (Grand Rapids, MI: Baker, 2008), 12.

7. The Pew Forum on Religion and Public Life, "United States Religious Landscape Survey," February 2008, 7.

8. Using the average United States resident's life expectancy of 79, as calculated by the CIA World Factbook. Accessed at http://en.wikipedia.org/wiki/Life_expectancy.

9. The Pew Forum on Religion and Public Life, "United States Religious Landscape Survey," February 2008, 81–82.

10. From within a group of 100 evangelicals and their 200 overtly secular counterparts.

11. Terry Whalin, *Luis Palau* (Minneapolis: Bethany House, 1996), 133.

12. "Mohammed, Britain's Most Popular Boy's Name in 2009," *Huffington Post*, October 27, 2010, http://www.huffingtonpost.com/2010/10/27/mohammed-britains -most-po_n_775145.html.

13. Heidi Blake, "Christian Preacher Arrested for Saying Homosexuality Is a Sin," *The Telegraph*, May 2, 2010, http://www.telegraph.co.uk/news/religion/7668448 /Christian-preacher-arrested-for-saying-homosexuality-is-a-sin.html.

14. Scott Thumma and Warren Bird, "National Survey of Megachurch Attendees," Hartford Institute for Religion and Research, 1.

15. Hartford Institute for Religion Research, http://hirr.hartsem.edu/research /fastfacts/fast_facts.html: "Most people attend larger churches" and "50 percent of churchgoers attended the largest 10 percent of congregations (350 regular participants and up)."

16. David T. Olson, *The American Church in Crisis* (Grand Rapids, MI: Zondervan, 2008), 43.

17. Ibid.

18. "State Population Growth 2000 to 2005, Based Upon United States Census Bureau Data. December 22, 2005." Access the downloadable PDF at: www.demographia.com/db-2005statepop.pdf.

19. Olson, *The American Church in Crisis*, 43.

20. "State Population Growth 2000 to 2005, Based Upon United States Census Bureau Data. December 22, 2005."

21. Olson, *The American Church in Crisis*, 43.

22. Christine Wicker, *The Fall of the Evangelical Nation* (New York: Harper One, 2008), 64–65.

23. Sarah Pulliam Bailey, "Q & A: Billy Graham on Aging, Regrets, and Evangelicals," *Christianity Today*, January 21, 2011, http://www.christianitytoday.com /ct/2011/januaryweb-only/qabillygraham.html. Used by permission.

24. George Barna, *Revolution* (Carol Stream, IL: BarnaBooks, 2005), 32.

25. Brad Waggoner, *The Shape of Faith to Come* (Nashville: B & H Books, 2008), as quoted by Ed Stetzer, "Future Trends in Evangelicalism," Patheos.com, http://www.patheos.com/Resources/Additional-Resources/Future-Trends-in-Evan gelicalism.html.

Chapter 7: Re-Valuing

1. George Barna, *Futurecast* (Carol Stream, IL: BarnaBooks, 2011), 200.

2. As quoted by Tim Stafford, "Watching Her Tone," *Christianity Today*, October 13, 2009, http://www.christianitytoday.com/ct/2009/october/24.96.html.

3. For this book I have coined the term "21st-Century Evangelical" as a positive label for those who remain committed to historic and orthodox evangelical theology and who are also eager to "course-correct" the American church to better be Christ's presence in this rapidly changing age.

4. Christian Missionary Alliance, http://www.cmalliance.org/about/history/tozer.

Chapter 8: Good

1. Phone interview, December 9, 2011. Steph's actual name has not been used, to protect her identity.

2. Jordi Gasso, "Controversial Minister Draws Outcry," *Yale Daily News*, April 1, 2011, http://www.yaledailynews.com/news/2011/apr/01/controversial-minister-draws-outcry/.

3. "Letter: Why We Invited Christopher Yuan," *Yale Daily News*, April 5, 2011, http://www.yaledailynews.com/news/2011/apr/05/letter-why-we-invited-christopher-yuan/.

4. Ibid.

5. Ben Prawdzik, "Minister's Message Divides Audiences," *Yale Daily News*, April 3, 2011, http://www.yaledailynews.com/news/2011/apr/03/ministers-message-divides -audiences/.

6. Charles Spurgeon, *Morning and Evening* (Peabody, MA: Hendrickson, 1991), 182.

7. Quoted by David Kinnaman and Gabe Lyons, *UnChristian* (Grand Rapids, MI: Baker, 2007), 234.

Chapter 9: Uniting

1. Jeffrey Kluger, "When Animals Attack—and Defend,"*Time* magazine, June 7, 2007, http://www.time.com/time/health/article/0,8599,1630667,00.html.

2. Mark Galli, "The Confidence of the Evangelical," *Christianity Today*, November 17, 2011, http://www.christianitytoday.com/ct/2011/novemberweb-only/confidence evangelical.html.

3. Francis Schaeffer, *The Great Evangelical Disaster* (Wheaton, IL: Crossway, 1984), 106. Used by permission of Crossway, a publishing ministry of Good News Publishers, Wheaton, IL 60187, www.crossway.org.

4. Albert Mohler, excerpted with permission from *Four Views on the Spectrum of Evangelicalism* (Grand Rapids, MI: Zondervan, 2011). Quoted at http://www.albertmohler .com/2011/09/26/a-new-third-way-reformist-evangelicals-and-the-evangelical-future/.

5. Ibid.

Chapter 10: Solvent

1. Laura Ortberg Turner, *Hermeneutics*, October 5, 2011, http://blog.christiani-tytoday.com/women/2011/10/john_ortberg_is_my_dad_but_don.html.

2. Scripture does present precedent for financially supporting Christian "workers," particularly those who teach and preach, in 1 Timothy 5:17–18. Scripture also models dedicated "tent-making" workers like the apostle Paul.

3. Biblical Stewardship, http://biblicalstewardship.net/statistical-research-on -stewardship/, which cites Bill Bright, quoted by Ron Blue in *Generous Living* (Grand Rapids, MI: Zondervan, 1997), 201, and Larry Eskridge, *Defining Evangelicalism* (Wheaton, IL: Institute for the Study of American Evangelicals, n.d.).

4. John J. Havens and Paul G. Schervish, "Why the $41 Trillion Wealth Transfer Estimate Is Still Valid: A Review of Challenges and Questions," *The Journal of Gift Planning* 7 (January 2003): 11–15, 47–50.

5. Blue, *Generous Living*, 201.

6. George Barna, *How to Increase Giving in Your Church* (Ventura, CA: Regal Books, 1997), 20.

7. Barna Group, April 14, 2008, http://www.barna.org/barna-update/article/18 -congregations/41-new-study-shows-trends-in-tithing-and-donating, and Barna Group, June 5, 2001, http://www.barna.org/barna-update/article/5-barna-update/51-churches -lose-financial-ground-in-2000.

8. John L. Ronsvalle and Sylvia Ronsvalle, *The State of Church Giving Through 2000* (Champaign, IL: empty tomb, inc., 2002), 51.

Chapter 11: Healing

1. Kenda Creasy Dean, *Almost Christian: What the Faith of Our Teenagers Is Telling the American Church* (Oxford: Oxford University Press, 2010), 4.

2. David Kinnaman, *You Lost Me* (Grand Rapids, MI: Baker, 2011), 13.

3. George Barna, *Futurecast* (Carol Stream, IL: BarnaBooks, 2011), 183.

4. Richard J. Krejcir, "What Is Going On With Pastors in America?" Schaeffer Institute, http://www.intothyword.org/apps/articles/default.asp?articleid=36562.

5. Quotes from Youth Transition Network founder, Jeff Schadt, in a two-hour phone interview. Schadt quoted United States evangelical teens on why they eventually give up on Christianity.

6. Asaph, a vocational worship leader, felt the common pressures of ministry, as recorded in Psalm 73:14–15: "All day long I have been plagued; I have been punished every morning. If I had said, 'I will speak thus,' I would have betrayed your children." His solution was to enter the presence of God, v. 17. Moses also insisted on the presence of God as the only means for ministry (Exodus 33:15). This is our only place of healing today.

7. The Great Commandment in Matthew 22:36–40 and Mark 12:30–31, as well as the Twelve's focus in Acts 6:3–4: "We will give this responsibility over to them and will give our attention to prayer and the ministry of the word." Also, see Acts 20:28.

8. John 15.

9. John 13.

10. Ephesians 4:11.

11. Also see God's foreshadowing in the shepherd King David and various Old Testament prophets.

12. Survey cited in: Ted Olsen, "Go Figure," *Christianity Today*, September 30, 2009, http://www.christianitytoday.com/ct/2009/october/10.68.html.

Chapter 12: Re-Igniting

1. Ed Stetzer, "Future Trends in Evangelicalism," *Patheos*, August 2, 2010, http://www. patheos.com/Resources/Additional-Resources/Future-Trends-in-Evangelicalism.html.

2. I thank God for notable exceptions to this, including Luis Palau and Greg Laurie, who are both being used by God in powerful ways.

3. Mark Dever and C. J. Mahaney, *The Gospel and Personal Evangelism* (Wheaton, IL: Crossway, 2007), 47.

4. John Stott, *Personal Evangelism* (Downers Grove, IL: InterVarsity Press, 1949), 3–4, as quoted by Mark Dever and C. J. Mahaney, *The Gospel and Personal Evangelism* (Wheaton, IL: Crossway, 2007), 47.

5. Ed Stetzer, "Proselytizing in a Multi-Faith World," *Christianity Today*, March 28, 2011, http://www.christianitytoday.com/ct/2011/april/proselytizingmultifaith.html.

Appendix C

1. Alister McGrath, *Evangelicalism and the Future of Christianity* (Downers Grove, IL: InterVarsity Press, 1995), 22.

2. David W. Bebbington, *Evangelicalism in Modern Britain: A History from the 1730s to the 1980s* (London: Unwin Hyman, 1989), 2–17; Mark A. Noll, *The Rise of Evangelicalism: The Age of Edwards, Whitefield, and the Wesleys* (Downers Grove, IL: InterVarsity Press, 2003), 19.

3. Bebbington, *Evangelicalism in Modern Britain*, 2–17.

4. Francis Schaeffer, *The Great Evangelical Disaster* (Wheaton, IL: Crossway, 1984), 97.

5. Christian Smith, *American Evangelicalism, Embattled and Thriving* (Chicago: The University of Chicago Press, 1998), 16.

6. Ibid.

Acknowledgments

Thank you to all who have invested and believed in this unlikely author. John McCandlish Phillips, mentor and friend. Steve Strickbine, dear friend and newspaper editor. Amy Silverman, the most gifted wordsmith I know. Dr. Roger Ball, who models the best ideals in this book. Terry and Carleen Moore, who funded much of my undergraduate studies. Diane Hakala, who funded my MDiv studies at Phoenix Seminary. Wes Yoder, agent extraordinaire. The amazing team at Baker, including Jon Wilcox, Ruth Anderson, Mike Cook, Jeff Braun, and Anna Scianna. Betty Solomon, Sarah Bright, Tom and Lynn Garasha, John Mark and Holly Kehlenbeck, Joey Coffman, Mom and Dad, Dr. Dan Dickerson, my loved ones at Cornerstone, my faithful and reliable team of disciples, and many others who deserve credit for anything good in this book.

More than anyone else, thank you to my confidant, partner, and best friend, Melanie. You surrendered many nights and weekends because you believe this message is bigger and more important than we are. You carry the weight of it with me. Thank you for your sacrifices.

John S. Dickerson is a nationally awarded journalist and third-generation senior pastor. In 2008, Tom Brokaw, Charles Gibson (ABC News), Michele Norris (NPR), and Anna Quindlen (*Newsweek*) selected him as winner of the Livingston Award for Young Journalists. He serves at Cornerstone, an Evangelical Free Church in Prescott, Arizona, where he lives with his wife and children. Learn more at JohnSDickerson.com.

For More Resources About

THE GREAT EVANGELICAL RECESSION

Visit JohnSDickerson.com

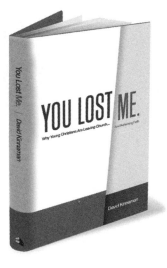